ARCHITECTURE OF THE EARTH

ENSAMBLE STUDIO

First published in Japan on June 8, 2021
Second published on February 10, 2022

Author Ensamble Studio:
             Antón García-Abril & Débora Mesa

Publisher Takeshi Ito
TOTO Publishing (TOTO LTD.)
TOTO Nogizaka Bldg., 2F
1-24-3 Minami-Aoyama, Minato-ku
Tokyo 107-0062, Japan
[Sales]   Telephone +81-3-3402-7138
             Facsimile +81-3-3402-7187
[Editorial] Telephone +81-3-3497-1010
URL https://jp.toto.com/publishing

Book design spread (Tomoko Sakamoto & David Lorente)

Print Sannichi Printing Co., Ltd.

Printed in Japan
ISBN 978-4-88706-390-7

ARCHITECTURE OF THE EARTH

大地の建築

ENSAMBLE STUDIO

アンサンブル・スタジオ

TABLE OF CONTENTS　　　　目次

ARCHITECTURE OF THE EARTH

Antón García-Abril & Débora Mesa

Architecture comes from the Earth. Metals, minerals, fibers, oil and soil that make up the Earth's crust get extracted, combined, and transformed. From land to building. For thousands of years, this process was straightforward: tree trunks made frames, mud made bricks, and stones made walls, arches and domes. Subtle traces remains of the architectures built with such technologies. With time, most of them disintegrate, eroded by water, burnt by the sun, blown by wind, and quaked by the earth. But in the past hundred years, this process has ultimately become a web of intricate and energy consuming actions—and reactions—that can no longer be narrowed down to a direct sequence of the kind 'a tree is cut and a hut is built'. Often, transformation happens to a point where the raw material is no longer recognizable. A rock becomes a thin tile; black petroleum, a glossy plastic sheet; sand, an invisible crystal. Matter displaces and travels globally, detached from its source, which is often exploited to the point of depletion, then abandoned, then replaced. But while our design decisions have significant impacts on the environment, we rarely pay attention to how, as we give shape to architecture, we reshape the Earth itself, which is a much greater architectural enterprise that escapes our competence.

WEATHERING

Revisiting the remains of megalithic constructions that we have encountered so many times across the Galician landscapes, we cannot help but wonder what will become of modern buildings and cities a few centuries from now. Today, ancient dolmens and castros built over two to three thousand years ago blend in with the landscape. They have lost the function they were originally made for, but they have come to terms with their weathering, and acquired a new meaning in their assimilation into their surrounding environment. But with so many layers, systems and mechanisms, it is hard to imagine contemporary constructions dissolving back into the earth to enrich its strata, brought back by Mother Nature. Whether we will be able to engineer some form of restoration of the appropriated resources, or build a new nature out of our own construction debris, the future is uncertain. What is clear is that being an architect today entails an added responsibility which requires gaining agency, recovering the contact with the means and methods that make architecture, and assuming the liability implied in such gains. Designing better and building better cannot happen without such commitment.

大地の建築

アントン・ガルシア＝アブリル ＆ デボラ・メサ

建築は地球から生まれる。地殻を構成する金属、鉱物、繊維、油、土が抽出され、結合され、変容する。大地から建築へ。何千年もの間、このプロセスは単純明快だった。木の幹が骨組みになり、泥がレンガになり、石が壁やアーチやドームになった。そういった技術を用いて構築された建築は、わずかな痕跡しか残されていない。時が経つにつれ、そのほとんどは崩壊し、水に侵食され、太陽に焼かれ、風に吹き飛ばされ、大地に揺さぶられた。しかし、過去100年の間に、このプロセスは「木を伐り、小屋を建てる」というような直接的な物事の連関に還元できない、エネルギーを大量に消費する行為と反応が交錯する複雑な網目構造に、最終的になってしまった。多くの場合、原材料はもはや認識できないほど変容する。岩は薄いタイルになり、黒い石油は光沢のあるプラスチックになり、砂は透明なガラスになる。物質は動かされ、世界中を旅し、その源から引き離され、多くの場合は枯渇するまで利用され、それから放棄され、別のものに置き換えられる。しかし、私たち建築家の設計上の判断が環境に甚大な影響を与える一方で、建築を形にするときに、どのように地球そのものを再構築するかという自分の力量を超えたはるかに大きな建築の企てに注意を払うことは、ほとんどない。

風化する

ガリシアの風景のなかで何度も遭遇した巨石建造物を再訪すると、数世紀後に現代の建築や都市はどうなっているだろうかと考えずにはいられない。数千年前に建てられたケルト人の支石墓や要塞は、今ではその土地に溶け込んでいる。それらは本来の機能を果たせなくなったが、風化を受け入れ、環境と同化することで新しい意味を得た。しかし、あまりに多くのレイヤー、システム、機構をもつ現代の建築が、母なる自然に呼び戻され、地球に溶け込み、大地を豊かにしていくとは想像しがたい。人間が

奪い取った資源を何らかのかたちで復元することができるのか、あるいは私たちがつくった建物の瓦礫から新しい自然を築くことができるのか、先は見えない。今日建築家であるということは、主体性を獲得し、建築をつくる手段や方法との連関を取り戻し、それらから生じるさらなる責任を必然的に負うことを意味する。このような深い関与なしには、より良い設計、より良い建築は実現できない。

EXPLOITING

When we decided to recycle materials from a quarry back in 2006, instead of using stone catalog products offered by suppliers to build the SGAE Headquarters, we found no other way to make this happen but to assume the risk of construction, that is, to become the contractors of the work. In all honesty, we did not approach the quarry with this idea. We just wanted to start the design of a project that had to use stone -by code- from a place where the stone is still part of the mountain, its potential, intact. We were overwhelmed by the brutality of the spectacle, the noise, the dust, and the synchronized explosions that changed the physiognomy of the Earth block by block in front of our eyes. Out of every squared rock, similar amount of non-squared material was deemed unusable and discarded. The lack of symmetry and regularity made it unfit for the subsequent processing operations, but we found great beauty in it. Using the discarded instead of cutting new material made complete sense to us, but paradoxically, it made sense just to us. Others saw liability where we saw opportunity. Because of the unconventionality of the occurrence we figured out no way

to implement it except to assume all consequences. And we did. During four months, we moved our gravity center to a quarry in Salceda de Caselas to work hand-in-hand with the quarry workers. Design materialized through trial-and-error, and through a true collaboration between experienced hands and ingenious minds. We built a full prototype close to the material source, and succeeded to minimize the uncertainty of the undertaking, before moving each and every stone to the city. The building that reassembles these rocks refers to the landscape, to the industrial, to the megalithic. It reads as a building but yet there is something that transcends the building and its surrounding context, that creates a visceral link between the material and its source.

LIBERATING

Working in urban contexts, we found ourselves subject to the abstract regulations of codes, the references given by human-made environments, our own education as Spanish architects within a European culture and Occidental perspective. It is only when we have worked outside such constraining contexts that we have met Nature and its potential to influence architecture beyond prescriptive models and methods. Liberated from urban patterns, grids, norms, forms, structures and infrastructures, we found the freedom to be inspired by landforms, constellations, geology, climate, and wilderness. Here we have set ourselves the task to design with the land, for the land, to enable architecture and artifice to coexist with it, without exploitation. Here, our mission becomes rediscovering the architecture of the Earth, and search for that materiality that connects us again and in a deep way with our environment, without cultural or normative layers, from the intimate connection that as human

最大限活用する

「スペイン著作権協会本部」を建設するために、2006年にメーカーのカタログから入手できる石材製品を用いずに採石場の材料を再利用すると決めたとき、これを実現する唯一の方法は、現場での工事リスクを負うこと、つまり施工者として工事を請け負うことだった。正直なところ、私たちはこのような考えがあって採石場に声をかけたわけではなかった。ただ、石材の使用が法規で定められていたプロジェクトを、石が山として存在し、その可能性が手つかずのまま保たれている場所から始めたかっただけだ。私たちは現場の光景の荒々しさ、騒音、粉塵、同時に起こる爆発が大きな塊を一つひとつ破壊し、私たちの目の前で地球が様相を変えていく様子に圧倒された。四角い岩の塊を切り出すたびに、同じぐらいの量の不整形の材料が使用不可能とみなされ、廃棄されていた。左右非対称で不規則な形だったため、その後の処理作業には適していなかったが、私たちはそこに大いなる美を見いだした。新しい材料を切り出す代わりに廃棄されたものを使うことは、私たちにとって理にかなっていたが、逆説的に言うなら、それが理にかなっていると考えたのは、私たちだけだった。私たちはすばらしい機会と捉えたが、ほかの人たちは不利だと考えた。あまりに型破りな試みだったので、私たちがすべての責任を負う以外にこれを実行する方法は考えられなかった。そして、私たちはそれを実行した。4か月の間、私たちは活動拠点をサルセダ・デ・カセラスの採石場に移し、採石場の作業員と手を取り合って働いた。行動し、試行錯誤しながら、経験豊富な手と創意工夫に満ちた思考の真の連携を通して設計が行われた。私たちは材料の供給源の近くに実物大のプロトタイプを構築することによって、一つひとつの石を市内に移送する前に、この難しい仕事にともなう不安要素を最小限に抑えることができた。これらの岩を再び組み上げた建物は、土地の景観、産業、そして巨石遺跡を表している。それは建物のように見えるが、そこには建物とその周辺環境を超越した、材料とその源の間に感覚的なつながりをもたらす何かが存在する。

解放する

私たちは都市的コンテクストのなかで仕事をしていると、自分たちが法規の抽象的な規制、人間がつくった環境から与えられるレファレンス、ヨーロッパ文化と西洋的なものの見方のなかでスペイン人建築家として受けた教育の影響を受けていることに気づく。このような制約の多いコンテクストの外で仕事をしてみて、初めて私たちは自然、そしてあらかじめ規定された模範や方法を超えて建築に影響を与えることができるその潜在的な可能性に出合うことができた。都市のパターン、グリッド、規範、形態、構造、インフラから解放されて、私たちは地形、星座、地質や気候、手つかずの自然からインスピレーションを得る自由を見いだした。私たちはここで、搾取することなく、建築や人工物が大地と共存できるように、大地を使って大地のために設計するという任務を自分たちに課した。ここでの私たちの使命は、私たち人間と私たちを支えてくれる土地との親密なつな

beings we have with the land that supports us. We understand this architecture as one that surrenders to matter and learns from it, without the urge to impose its dogmas, treatises or systems on the logic of the Earth.

EXPLORING

The first impulses of this desire to find the architecture of the Earth, emerged more than a decade ago with The Truffle, an experiment that broke canons and instigated the search for an unprecedented way of conceiving architecture. Attracted by the mighty Atlantic landscape in Costa da Morte, and inspired to build a space in that landscape, we approached the project as a reorganization of local matter that made intensive use of existing resources. We trusted that the encounter between neighbor materials, their physical and chemical reactions, would produce a result that would be greater than the sum of its parts. What we obtained far exceeded our most exigent expectations. Poetry and pragmatism appeared in communion. We had built an inhabitable space with structural integrity, thermal performance, and domestic functionality, relinquishing control over form, texture and detail, in order to let matter speak for itself. Architecture was able to refer to the land as if it was an extension of it. And a new idea of beauty emerged. The resulting ambiguities were multiple and captivating.

The intuitive action that guided the construction of The Truffle uncovered a path that led us to Structures of Landscape. A few years later and in another sublime context located north of Yellowstone National Park, we relaunched our investigations in one of the most geologically active regions on our planet. This geography, vast, wild, and earthy, opens up a new horizon. Beyond the scale of the building, we look at the territory and use constellations as the system of order that can help us articulate areas of special intensity within the immensity of space. And while the sky gets printed on the land to give it order, architecture takes geology as reference to create structure and form. Valleys, mountains, hills, canyons, and geysers offer an infinite source for interpretation, and erosion, fragmentation, crystallization, explosion... become the constructive processes that inform the design. Design materialized through action, and it cannot be possible otherwise. Our hands and senses come together to manipulate matter through the material, formal and expressive possibilities we find in the place. Models, mock-ups and prototypes help to develop ideas and the training to realize them. Through a malleable and flexible process, they incarnate the architectures that await the moment to be linked to a place, endowed with a scale, and transformed into space as a nexus between humans and Earth.

がりのなかから、地球の建築を再発見し、文化や規範などのレイヤーなしに、深いかたちで私たちを環境と再び結びつける物質性を探求することである。私たちはこの建築の信条、理論、システムを地球の理に押し付けようとはしない。私たちは、地球の理にこの建築の信条、理論、システムを押し付けたいといった衝動に駆られることなく、物質に身を委ね、物質から学ぶ建築としてそれを理解する。

探求する

初めて地球の建築を見つけたいと強く感じたのは、10年以上前に、規範を覆す新しい建築の考え方を探求するきっかけとなった実験である「トリュフ」に取り組んだときだった。コスタ・ダ・モルテの壮大な大西洋の風景に魅せられて、その風景の一部として空間を構築したいという着想を得た私たちは、それを深く考えるために、既存の資源を集中的に活用し、地域の材料を再編する試みとしてこのプロジェクトに取り組んだ。私たちは、隣り合う材料どうしの出合いとそれらの物質的・化学的反応によって、それらを合わせたもの以上の結果が生まれることを信じていた。私たちが得たものは、私たちのもっとも切実にかなえたいことの期待をはるかに超えていた。詩と実用主義が共存していた。私たちは、物質自体に語らせるために、形態、質感、ディテールのコントロールを手放し、構造的な完全性、熱性能、生活機能を備えた居住可能な空間を構築した。実際に、その建築はまるで地面の延長であるかのような様相を見せていた。そして、新しい美の概念が生まれた。結果として生じた曖昧さは、多面的で魅力的だった。

「トリュフ」の建設を進めた直感的な行動が、私たちを「ランドスケープの構造体」へ続く道に導いた。数年後、私たちは地球上でもっとも地質学的に活発な地域のひとつであるイエローストーン国立公園の北にある雄大な環境において調査を再開した。この広大な野生の大地で新しい地平線を見いだす。建物のスケールを超えて、この地域に目を向け、広大な宇宙の中にある、特別な強度をもつ地域を明確にするための手助けをしてくれる秩序の体系として星座を用いる。映し出された空は野生の大地に秩序を与え、地形は建築に構造と形をもたらす手がかりとなる。谷、山、丘、峡谷、間欠泉はさまざまな解釈を無限に生み出す源となる。そして侵食、断片化、結晶、爆発……は、設計を示唆する施工プロセスになる。そして行動しながら設計が行われる。それ以外のやり方はできない。私たちは手と頭を同時に働かせて、物質を巧みに操り、材料、形態や表現の新しい可能性を見いだす。模型、モックアップ、プロトタイプを使ってアイディアを高め、それらを実現するための練習を行う。可塑的で自由なプロセスを通して、それらは場所とつながり、スケールを与えられ、人間と地球の結節点としての空間となる瞬間を待つ建築を具現化する。

EARTHING AND UNEARTHING

The inventiveness and spontaneity of the creative process is carried out through construction, where the earth becomes an inseparable partner. Land holds, land molds, land mixes, land warms and protects the structures until they are ready to be unearthed, discovered, and inhabited. The architectures obtained are not perfect or immaculate, but rough and unrefined. They are ancient and new at the same time. They bear the prints of the land that was molded to give them form, and synthesize the accidents that occur on them, seeking the emotions that the contemplation of nature evokes. From the intimate contact between architecture and its ground, a direct link is forged. This connection is what makes works such as Truffle and Structures of Landscape reach a deep communion with the natural environment, and the evocation that keeps our pulse to develop this architecture on a different scale and in different locations. The hills of Calderona, the desert of the Arabian peninsula, the park on Governors Island in New York City, or the Irish National War Memorial Gardens in Dublin, give us new grounds to work with, further exploring the relationship between architecture and nature.

INHABITING

Once built, they belong. This is their dexterity. The Earth takes them and affects them over time. At the same time they create an inhabitable space where there was none before.

Such architectures can be created from scratch, where there is no shelter, no shade, no home. But they also exist unnoticed, awaiting their rescue. Ca'n Terra was discovered. Manually mined without architecture in mind, it is, enigmatically, one of the most magnificent spaces we have ever encountered. Finding Ca'n Terra in the guts of the Earth and disregarding its abandonment, deterioration and dirt to determine its inherent value, was the first design action of this project. This was also the most humble and most relevant design decision made. Others followed. Light, water, air and fire became our construction materials to revive the dormant space with sensible intervention.

To live in harmony with this project and enjoy an immersive experience, Ensamble moves its center of gravity to Ca'n Terra, which becomes a laboratory, a house, and an exploited land all at the same time. Once again, we find ourselves in a quarry that was confronted by human and natural forces. From the depth of a mine that presents us with a found space, we aspire to receive the whisper that guides us into this search, isolated and protected from all the disturbances of the cultural and architectural world. There, with our hands, we search in our creative subconscious, the architectures that the Earth allows, and that we bring to life.

土に埋める、
土から掘り出す

なくてはならない協力者である地球とともに工事を進めるなかで、創造的なプロセスにおける発想力や臨機応変さだけが頼りだった。構造物が掘り起こされ、見いだされ、すみかとなる準備が整うまで、土はそれを保持し、成形し、混ぜ合わせ、温め、保護する。そこから得た建築は、完全でも完璧でもない。荒々しく粗野だ。古いと同時に新しい。それらは、それらに形を与えた大地の痕跡を留め、それらが築かれる過程で起こったさまざまな偶然の出来事を統合し、自然についての思索が引き起こすさまざまな感情を探し求めている。建築と大地の密接な関わりから、直接的なつながりが生まれる。この繋がりは、「トリュフ」や「ランドスケープの構造体」のような作品を自然環境と深く結びつけ、この建築をさまざまなスケールや場所で展開したいという私たちの熱意を鼓舞し続けてくれる。カルデローナの丘、アラビアの砂漠、ニューヨークのガバナーズ・アイランドの公園、ダブリンのアイルランド国立戦争記念碑庭園は、私たちに建築と自然の関係をさらに探りつつ建築に取り組むための新たな場所を与えてくれる。

すみかとする

いったん構築されると、建築はその場所の重要な一部になる。これが建築の巧妙さだ。地球はそれらを取り込み、時間が経つにつれてそれらに影響を及ぼすと同時に、前には何もなかったところにすみかとなる空間をつくり出す。

そのような建築物は、雨風を避ける覆いも日陰も家もないところに、ゼロからつくることができる。そして、それらは誰にも気づかれずに存在し、救け出されるのを待っている。「カン・テラ」が発見された。建築にするつもりはなく無作為に人の手で採掘されていたそれは、不思議なことに、私たちが今まで出合ったなかでもっとも壮大な空間のひとつだった。地球の奥深くに埋もれていた「カン・テラ」を発見し、その放棄され、荒廃し、埃にまみれた外観にとらわれずに、そこに潜在的な価値を見いだしたことが、このプロジェクトの最初

の設計行為だった。それはもっとも謙虚で、もっとも的確な設計行為でもあった。そしてほかのことが次々と起こった。光、水、空気、火は私たちの建築材料になり、思慮深い介入によって、眠っていた空間に命が吹き込まれた。

この建築と一体となった生活を送り、没入的な経験を楽しむために、アンサンブル・スタジオは、実験場、家、そして最大限活用される土地であるカン・テラに活動の中心を移した。私たちは再び、人間と自然の力が対峙する採石場にいる。自然の恵みとして見いだされた空間を私たちに与えてくれた鉱山の奥底から、私たちは文化的・建築的な世界のあらゆる妨害から隔離され、守られながら、この探求を導いてくれる囁きに耳を傾けたいと熱望している。そこで私たちは自分たちの手を使って、創造的な潜在意識のなかで、地球が受け入れてくれる建築、私たちの大地の建築を探し求める。

Our first works take us to Galicia, a region in the north of Spain with extensive rural land, powerful coastal landscape, Atlantic climate, and memorable architectures that span from prehistoric to present times.

In Santiago de Compostela, the historic city par excellence, we built two buildings in the same garden, 3 years apart. The Musical Studies Center and SGAE Headquarters are neighbors in Vista Alegre Park, one of the most prominent green areas near the historic center of the city. It was masterplanned by architects Arata Isozaki and Cesar Portela at the closure of the century and was programmed to accommodate academic buildings, intended for the training of the Galician Orchestra musicians.

Our encounter with stone as a construction material comes as a result of working in this geography, which is rich in granite, and also applying zoning regulations that dictate what is buildable in the historic center of the city and the surrounding areas.

初期の一連の作品は、広大な田園地帯、力強い海岸の風景、太西洋の気候、そして先史時代から現在までの記憶に残る建築物があるスペイン北部のガリシア地方へ、私たちを誘う。

すばらしい歴史的都市のサンティアゴ・デ・コンポステーラで、私たちは同じ庭園に2つの建築を3年の間隔をあけて建てた。「音楽高等学校」と「スペイン著作権協会本部」は、この街の歴史的中心部に近い有名な緑地、ヴィスタ・アレグレ公園内に隣り合わせに位置する。20世紀末に建築家の磯崎新とセザール・ポルテラによりマスタープランが作成され、ガリシア交響楽団の音楽家の養成を目的とした教育施設が計画された。

私たちが建築材料としての石と出合ったのは、花崗岩が豊富なこの土地で仕事をしたからだった。また、都市の歴史的中心部やその周辺に建てられる建築を規定するゾーニング規制によって、石でつくることが決められていたからでもある。

MUSICAL STUDIES CENTER

音楽高等学校

Santiago de Compostela, Spain 2003

スペイン、サンティアゴ・デ・コンポステーラ

17

It is impossible for us to walk on the streets of Santiago de Compostela or to visit the megalithic remains that inhabit the Galician countryside and limit our architectural contribution to the use of the highly processed products offered by commercial stone catalogs.

The need to build with a material, granite, which we did not know much about, but which offered possibilities beyond those that the industry exploits in our eyes, us to a local quarry in Salceda de Caselas. There we discovered the contemporary potential of stone beyond conventional applications.

私たちはサンティアゴ・デ・コンポステーラの道を歩き、ガリシアの田園地帯に点在する巨石遺跡を訪ねて、ここで建築をつくるのに、石材メーカーのカタログの製品を使うことなどあり得ないと考えた。

花崗岩という私たちにとってあまり馴染みのない、しかし産業界で利用されている以上の可能性がありそうな素材を使って建築をつくる必要に迫られて、私たちはサルセダ・デ・カセラスの採石場にやってきた。ここで私たちは、従来の用途を超えた石の現代的な可能性を発見した。

Our architectural investigations with stone are informed by a set of contrasting references, like the prehistoric settlements that dot the coastal landscapes of A Coruña, the historic architectures of the city of Santiago de Compostela, or the industrial processes that transform the material.

私たちの石をめぐる建築的調査は、ア・コルーニャの海岸沿いに見られるカストロ・デ・バローニャなどのケルト人の先史時代の集落の風景、サンティアゴ・デ・コンポステーラの歴史的な街並の建築、そして材料の加工プロセスを含む工業という異なる参考事例から情報を得ている。

The Musical Studies Center is one of the academic buildings that make up Vista Alegre Park. The competition brief invited architects to design a twin building next to the Center for Advanced Studies by architect César Portela. The location, volume and exterior materials to be used in the building were prescribed in order to guarantee the desired similarity between the two buildings.

Meeting these requirements while attempting to apply an exercise in asymmetry, the building is designed as a rock that has a will to be cubic, resting on the grass. It resembles the giant blocks that we saw at the quarry, neatly cut from the mountain using diamond wire and dynamite. It is built out of thick structural slabs sliced through the planes of natural stereotomy that makes the granite split open more easily. The face of the slab that bears the imprints of the drill bits becomes a facade, making the industrial process part of the architectural ornamentation.

This raw and massive exteriority gives way to a neutral and smooth interiority. Perforations integrated into the building's mass—in the form of windows, doors, corridors or lightwells—fill its core with natural light, and articulate programs based on acoustics and access. A lively environment resides inside this soundproof rock that quietly exists in the garden and expressively reacts with its abrasive texture to the whims of the Galician climate.

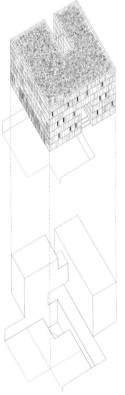

「音楽高等学校」は、ヴィスタ・アレグレ公園を構成する教育施設のひとつだ。コンペ概要では、建築家のセザール・ポルテラが設計した先進研究センターに隣接する2棟の建物の設計案が求められた。2棟の建物を同じような外観にすることが求められており、類似性を確保するために、配置、ボリューム、外装材はあらかじめ規定されていた。

これらの要件を満たすと同時にアシメトリーの構成を試みた結果、この建物は草の上に置かれたキューブのような岩として設計された。採石場にあった巨大な石の塊をダイアモンドワイヤーとダイナマイトを使って切り出し、再構成している。この建物は、花崗岩が自然に割れやすい面に沿ってスライスされた分厚い構造スラブでできている。掘削機の痕が残るスラブの表面がファサードになり、製造工程は建築の装飾の一部になる。

加工されていない重厚な外観は、ニュートラルで滑らかな内観に移行する。窓、扉、廊下、ライトウェルなどの形で建築のマスに組み込まれた孔を通って、自然光が建物の中を満たし、音響の条件や動線に基づいてプログラムが明確化される。庭の中に静かに佇む防音処理されたこの岩の中には活気に満ちた環境が存在し、その粗い質感は、ガリシア地方の気候の激しい変化に表情豊かに応えている。

Concept Drawing
コンセプトドローイング

A few meters away from the Musical Studies Center, the headquarters for the General Society of Authors and Editors (SGAE) is built in the same property, using material from the same nearby quarry. In this case, the experimentation with granite is taken a step further.

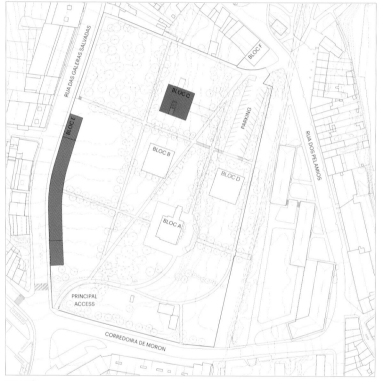

Site Plan
配置図

同じ敷地内の「音楽高等学校」から数メートル離れた場所に、近くの同じ採石場の石材を使った「スペイン著作権協会本部」が建つ。この建物では、花崗岩を使った実験をさらに一歩進めている。

SGAE HEADQUARTERS
スペイン著作権協会本部

Santiago de Compostela, Spain 2007

スペイン、サンティアゴ・デ・コンポステーラ

25

Quarries generate an abundance of waste materials, irregular rocks which result from cutting perfectly squared blocks. These gradually fill up the slopes and shoulders of the trucking lines that go up and down the mountain, awaiting the moment to be crushed, turned into gravel or dust. Much of these materials are robust, structurally sound, beautifully raw and also inexpensive because of their irregular shapes.

For the SGAE Headquarters, we took the challenge to create architecture with these leftover materials, and built a structural wall that recycles heterogeneous granite boulders. Such unconventional approach demands that we move to the quarry to work hand-in-hand with the stone experts, designing while building, and eventually building a full scale prototype that will resolve every detail and clear up most of the uncertainties before transporting it, stone by stone, to the final site.

採石場では、四角いブロックを切り出した後に残る不整形な岩石が廃材として大量に発生する。これらの廃棄物はトラックが山を上り下りする構内通路の斜面や路肩を徐々に埋め尽くし、砕け散って砂利や砂塵になる瞬間を待っている。この素材の大部分は頑丈で構造的にも一体性があり、未加工のままで美しい。そして形が崩れているので安価でもある。

「スペイン著作権協会本部」では、私たちはこの残った材料を使って建築をつくることに挑戦し、異なる形状の花崗岩の巨石を使って構造壁を構築した。このような型破りのアプローチを実践するために、私たちは採石場に拠点を移す必要があった。私たちは石工たちと手を取り合って働き、設計をしながら製作し、最後に石を最終的な敷地にひとつずつ運ぶ前に、すべてのディテールや不確定要素の大部分を解決するために実寸大のプロトタイプを製作した。

Process: Natural Stone Quarry
プロセス：天然石の採石場

Quarries are dusty and noisy, and are not the type of places anyone but a quarry worker would spend much time in, if at all visit. Still they are a direct reflection of the impact of design decisions on the environment.

採石場は埃っぽくて騒がしく、採石作業員以外の人にとっては、訪れたとしても長い時間を過ごすような場所ではない。それでも、採石場は設計上の判断が環境に与える影響を直接反映している場所だと思う。

In this quarry in Salceda de Caselas, we spent four months, day after day, learning, designing while building, and collaborating, as we figured out how to make architecture out of left-over materials.

サルセダ・デ・カセラスにあるこの採石場で、私たちは4か月過ごし、毎日学び、行動しながら設計し、共同作業を行った。残った材料から建築をつくる方法を考える。

Through physical models we started thinking about the process of building a self-supporting wall.

模型を使って、自立する壁を構築する工程を考えはじめた。

Building a prototype in the quarry was key to completing the design, the engineering process and to minimize the uncertainty on site. We started with a mock-up of a section and ended up assembling the full wall.

採石場でプロトタイプを構築することは、設計およびエンジニアリングのプロセスを完結させ、現場での不確定要素を最小限に抑えるための鍵となった。私たちはまず断面のモックアップからはじめて、最後に壁全体を組み立てた。

On the site, the building occupies the perimeter of the property, becoming part of the park's limit. It is planned as a sequence of three walls which run along a space of varied constructive, material and perceptive scales: a stone wall looking into the garden, an interior wall made of jewel boxes and a translucent glass wall facing the street. They all work as filters of different urban conditions delimiting and organizing the program in functional strips. The program includes social activities for the attendance of authors and publishers, as well as a wide range of public cultural activities distributed in four levels, with access from both the garden and the street. Three thousand square meters to serve the city and its artists.

The building arches, widens and narrows through interaction of its constructive elements, generating fluid multivalent spaces, like a porticoed street which evokes the city of Santiago and its urban public spaces. Walking through it, the building becomes an urban space inside a garden, which reactivates the site bringing vitality and dynamism. Towards the garden, the granite wall creates a symbolic link between the city and the industrial sites that feed it; between megalithic architectures and contemporary ones. Built with irregular rocks selected directly from the quarry's dump yard, this sculptural element causes the disintegration of the building as such, transcending its functional dimension within Vista Alegre Park.

敷地では、この建物は土地の境界線沿いに配置され、公園の境界の一部分を形成する。この建物は連続する壁として計画された。さまざまな施工方法、材料、知覚的スケールで構成される空間に沿って、3つの壁が設けられる。庭園に面した石の壁、再生材を積層した宝石のようにほのかに光る内壁、道路に面した半透明のガラス壁。それらはすべて、さまざまな都市の状況を取り込むフィルターとしての役割を果たし、プログラムはこれらの壁に沿って帯状に配置されている。機能としては、作家や出版社が参加する社会活動や4つの階に分散された幅広い地域の文化活動などに使用され、庭と道路の両方からのアクセスが設けられている。延床面積は3,000m²で、この街と芸術家たちのために建設された。

建物はその構成要素の相互作用によってアーチを描き、サンティアゴの街とその公共空間を思い起こさせるポルティコで覆われた街路のような流動的で多面的な空間をつくり出している。その中を歩くと、建物は庭の中の都市空間になり、敷地に新たな活気とダイナミズムが生まれる。庭に向かって、花崗岩の壁は都市とそれを支える工業地帯との間、そして巨石の建築と現代的な建築の間に象徴的なつながりを形成する。採石場の廃棄物集積所から直接選ばれた不整形な岩石を使って建てられたこの建築は、ヴィスタ・アレグレ公園の中の建築としての機能を全うしつつも、建築のイメージを壊すような彫刻的な存在感を放っている。

Our explorations on Galician territory extend from the city to the shore; from the urban terraces of Santiago de Compostela, to the rural grounds of Bergantiños.

In Costa da Morte—or Death Shore—we make our next stop, overwhelmed by the wilderness of nature: land, water and sky brutally collide in this section of the Atlantic coastline. On a rocky cliff, we find a plot of land with tall pine trees. It is a perfect place to rest quietly, while watching an ever-changing spectacle of color and light on the horizon, right where the water and the sky meet.

To frame this view, we built The Truffle, which is part architecture and part landscape.

私たちのガリシア地方の探検は、街から海岸へと広がっていく。サンティアゴ・デ・コンポステーラの街のテラスからベルガンティーニョスの田園地帯へ。

コスタ・ダ・モルテ (死の海岸) で、私たちは自然の荒々しさに圧倒され、立ち止まる。大西洋の海岸線のこの区間で、陸、水、空は猛々しくぶつかり合う。岩場の崖の上に、背の高い松の木が生えている土地を見つける。水と空が出合う水平線上で刻々と変化する色と光の圧倒的な光景を眺めながら静かに休むには、最適の場所だ。

この眺望を捉えるために、私たちは建築でもあり、風景でもある「トリュフ」を建てる。

THE TRUFFLE

トリュフ

Costa da Morte, Spain 2010

スペイン、コスタ・ダ・モルテ

The Truffle is a piece of nature built from earth, full of air. A space within a stone that sits on the ground and blends in with the territory. It camouflages by emulating the processes of mineral formation in its structure, and integrates with the natural environment, complying with its laws.

The architecture of The Truffle does not follow canonical rules in the way it is designed or built. There are no drawings or exact dimensions. Local materials—soil, rocks, hay bales, and vegetation are gathered, mixed and combined with concrete following a simple recipe that makes the best use of the resources nearby.

「トリュフ」は、たっぷりと空気をはらんだ土でできた自然の断片だ。石の中にある空間は地面の上に鎮座し、領域に溶け込んでいる。それは、自らの構造の中の鉱物形成のプロセスを模倣することによって自然の中に身を隠し、その法則に従いながら自然環境と一体化する。

「トリュフ」の建築は、設計や施工の正統なルールには従っていない。図面も正確な寸法もない。土、岩、干し草俵、植物など土地の材料が集められ、身の回りの資源を最大限に活かしたシンプルなやり方で、混ぜ合わされ、組み合わされる。

Process: the Construction of The Truffle
プロセス:「トリュフ」の施工

For the construction of the Truffle, we dug a hole in the ground, piling up along its perimeter the topsoil that had been removed. As a result, we were able to obtain a retaining dike without mechanical consistency in an economical manner.

「トリュフ」を施工するために、私たちは取り除いた表土を周りに積み上げながら、地面に穴を掘った。この方法で、一貫した機械的強度はもたないが経済的な型枠を確保した。

Our neighbor's hay bales became the perfect solution to building a big volume easily.

近所の農家の干し草俵が、簡単に大きなボリュームをつくるための最適な解決策となった。

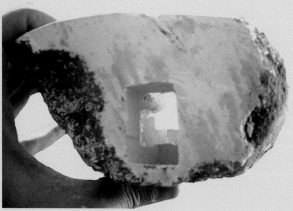

▶

We stacked them to
temporarily recreate the
volume of the interior
space, using this very
light mass.

この非常に軽い大きな塊を
積み上げて、一時的に内部空
間のボリュームをつくった。

We filled the space
between the earth and
the hay with concrete
to cast a structure. The
poured liquid wrapped
the hay and protected
itself with the soil.

地面と干し草の間にコンク
リートを流し込んで、構造体
を打設した。流し込んだコン
クリートは干し草を包み込
み、コンクリート自体は土で
保護された。

After a certain time had passed, we removed the soil to discover an amorphous mass. The earth and concrete exchanged their properties. The earth provided the concrete with its texture and color, its form and its essence, and the concrete gave the earth its strength and internal structure. But it was not yet architecture that we had created. We had made a stone.

時が経ち、土を取り除くと、不定形の量塊が現れた。土とコンクリートは、お互いの特性を交換し合った。土はコンクリートに質感と形、色、本質を与え、コンクリートは土に強度と内部構造を与えた。しかし、私たちがつくったものは、まだ建築ではなかった。私たちは石をつくったのだ。

Using quarrying machines, we made a few cuts to reach the core and the hay inside, compressed by the hydrostatic pressure exerted by the concrete on the flimsy vegetal structure.

採石機を使って、石の中心に到達するためにいくつか切れ込みを入れると、その中にコンクリートの静水圧で押しつぶされてぺちゃんこになった草の構造物を発見した。

To empty the interior, Paulina, the calf, was brought in and was treated to 50 m³ of the nicest food, which she fed on for a year until she left her habitat after growing to become a cow weighing 300 kg.

内部を空にするために、子牛のパウリーナがやってきて、50m³の最高に美味しい餌を楽しんだ。1年後にこのすみかを離れたときには、彼女はすでに体重300kgの成牛になっていた。

The interior volume had been eaten away, and the space appeared for the first time, revealing the architectural condition of The Truffle after having been a shelter for the animal and the hay bales for some time.

内部のボリュームが食べ尽くされ、初めて空間が現れ、しばらくの間、生い繁る植物と動物の隠れ家になっていた「トリュフ」は、建築としてよみがえった。

The resulting architecture surprised us. The ambiguity between the natural and the manufactured was intriguing, as intriguing was the complex materiality that the same constructive element—the unreinforced concrete mass—could provide the small architectural space at different scales. From the shapeless texture of its exterior, to the violent incision of a cut that reveals its architectural vocation, to the rusticated scale imprinted by the hay bales, and to the liquid expression of the ceiling that evokes the sea, and looks sublimely at the Atlantic Ocean, highlighting the horizon as the only tense line of the interior space.

その結果現れた建築は、私たちを驚かせた。自然と人工物の間の曖昧さに魅了され、無筋コンクリートという同じ構築要素がさまざまなスケールの建築空間にこれほど複雑な物質性をもたらしたことにも、同様に興味をかき立てられた。その形のない外観の質感から、建築としての使命を明らかに示す荒々しい切り口、内部で固化したコンクリートの流動的な表情に至るまで。干し草俵の大きさを反映した緻密な素材感は垂直な壁に素朴なスケール感を与え、天井面の海のような流動感とコントラストをなす。それらが石化してできた空間フレームの窓から大西洋を望めば、室内の唯一の緊張感を持ったラインとして水平線が際立って見える。

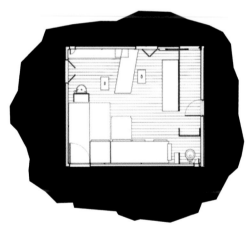
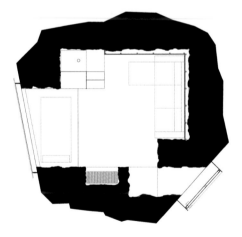

To provide the space with the comfort and the living conditions that architecture requires, we took Le Corbusier's "Cabanon" as a motif, recreating its program and dimensions.

建築に必要な快適さと生活条件をこの空間に与えるために、私たちはル・コルビュジエの「キャバノン」（カップ・マルタンの休暇小屋）をモチーフとして用いて、そのプログラムと寸法を再現した。

0   5 m

The lesson we learned was the uncertainty that led us in
the desire to build with our own hands, a piece of nature,
a contemplative space, a little poem.

私たちはここで、不確実性を学んだ。私たちは不確実性に導かれながら、
ひとかけらの自然、瞑想の空間、小さな詩を自分たちの手で構築したい
という強い願望を行動に移していった。

The Truffle is a seminal work for Ensamble Studio. We made it with a stroke of intuition, not at all anticipating the impact it would have in our research, in our understanding of what architecture is, and foremost, what it can be. It is with The Truffle that we "cultivate" a structure for the first time; that we elevate the beauty of imperfection, and uncover the excitement of relinquishing control during the creative process; that we design architecture and obtain landscape.

From this point, an unknown path is paved, and we walk on it to find other incredibly exciting destinations: from Structures of Landscape for Tippet Rise Art Center in Fishtail, Montana; to Petrified River for Cooper Hewitt Smithsonian Design Museum in New York City; to the Desert Rocks of AlUla, and beyond.

「トリュフ」は、アンサンブル・スタジオにとって重要な作品だ。私たちは直感に導かれてこの作品をつくったが、それが私たちの研究、そして建築とは何か、そして何になり得るかを理解する上でどんな影響を及ぼすことになるか、まったく予想していなかった。

「トリュフ」を通して、私たちは初めて建築を「育み」、不完全なものの美を高め、創造の過程でコントロールを手放すことのおもしろさを発見し、建築を設計して風景を手に入れる。

この地点から、見知らぬ道は踏み固められ、私たちはすばらしく刺激に満ちた目的地を目指して、その上を歩いていく。モンタナ州フィッシュテイルにあるティペット・ライズ・アート・センターのための「ランドスケープの構造体」から、ニューヨークシティのクーパー・ヒューイット国立デザイン博物館の「石化した川」、アル・ウラーの「砂漠の岩」、そしてその先へ。

STRUCTURES OF LANDSCAPE

ランドスケープの構造体

for Tippet Rise Art Center, Fishtail, Montana, USA 2016

米国、モンタナ州、フィッシュテイル、ティペット・ライズ・アート・センター

Located at the edge of Yellowstone National Park in Montana, Tippet Rise Art Center—set on a 12,000-acre working sheep and cattle ranch—was built as a new destination for the arts, in which music performances and large-scale outdoor sculptures play a major role.

How the current local fauna and ranching activity can coexist with the added artistic and architectural interventions was a challenge that the project embraced. This challenge has fueled a research that started with our early experiences in the quarry and continued with experiments like The Truffle, advancing the knowledge and appreciation of what pre-existing natural conditions can bring to us as architects and as users of architecture.

モンタナ州イエローストーン国立公園の端に位置するティペット・ライズ・アート・センターは、羊と牛の放牧地である12,000エーカー（約48.56km²）の敷地に位置し、音楽の演奏や大規模な野外彫刻を中心とする新しい芸術の発信地として誕生した。

現在この地域に生息する動物や牧場の活動が、新しい芸術的・建築的な介入といかに共存できるか。それがこのプロジェクトの課題だ。この課題は、初期の採石場での経験からはじまり、「トリュフ」などの実験を通して継続していた私たちの研究を加速させ、私たちが建築家として、そして建築のユーザーとして、既存の自然条件が私たちに何をもたらすかについての知識や理解を深めるきっかけとなった。

Thinking while making is the methodology used to design, guided by the intuition and sensibility of both our heads and our hands.

The physical model serves as the most suitable medium for design, where matter, structure and space are molded simultaneously.

つくりながら考えることは、
頭と手の直感と感性によって
導かれる設計手法だ。

模型は、物質、構造、空間が
同時に形成される、設計にもっ
とも適した媒体としての役割
を果たす。

Once again we go back to primary elements to configure site-specific architectures in harmony with nature. Working with earth, rocks, and learning from their formation logic, different techniques and processes are developed to manipulate the structural, acoustical and thermal properties of these local materials at different scales and geological transformation processes—sedimentation, erosion, weathering, crystallization, compaction, metamorphism—are reinterpreted to cultivate structures made of landscape from the landscape. Structures stir existing matter and reinforce it, using highly engineered processes while welcoming unpredictable results.

The forms obtained have been twinned with those taken from the land that previously contained and supported them when in state of rest, from which they retain memory and imprint and to which they introduce a new meaning and tension.

そうして得られたかたちは、かつて休止状態だったそれらを包含し、支持していた大地から取り出した形と組み合わされて、それらの中に宿り続ける記憶と痕跡をもたらした大地に新たな意味と緊張関係をもたらす。

自然と調和したサイト・スペシフィックな建築をつくるために、私たちはもう一度、原初の要素に立ち返る。土や岩石に向き合い、それらの形成の論理から学びながら、さまざまなスケールで土地の材料の構造、音響、熱の特性を操作するためのさまざまな技術やプロセスが考案される。そして、堆積、侵食、風化、結晶化、圧密、変成作用などの地殻変動のプロセスは、ランドスケープを材料として、ランドスケープから構築物を育むために再解釈される。構造体は予測不可能な結果を受け入れつつ、高度なプロセスを用いて、そこにある物質を攪拌し、補強する。

We call them Structures of Landscape because they are born from it and give it order, transforming matter into inhabitable space and unfolding a new constellation of programs among the plateaus, ridges, canyons and hills of brutal beauty that compose the site.

私たちは、それらのものを「ランドスケープの構造体」と呼ぶ。なぜなら、それらはランドスケープから生まれ、それに秩序を与え、物質を居住可能な空間に変換して、敷地を構成する荒々しい美に満ちた大地、尾根、峡谷、丘陵の間で新しいプログラムの集合体を展開するからだ。

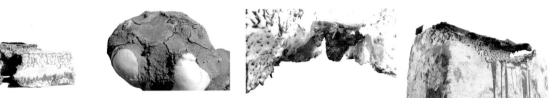

A series of 30 different architectures is created; each responding to a specific condition of the land; each made for a particular location; each serving a desired function. Each, a small node of a bigger masterplan that can be implemented throughout time. Each, a possible star of this earthly constellation.

30の異なる建築が次々と生み出される。それぞれが土地の固有の条件に応え、特定の場所のためにつくり出され、求められる機能を果たす。それぞれがいつでも実行可能な、大きなマスタープランのなかの小さな結節点だ。一つひとつが、この地上の星座を構成する可能性を秘めた星なのだ。

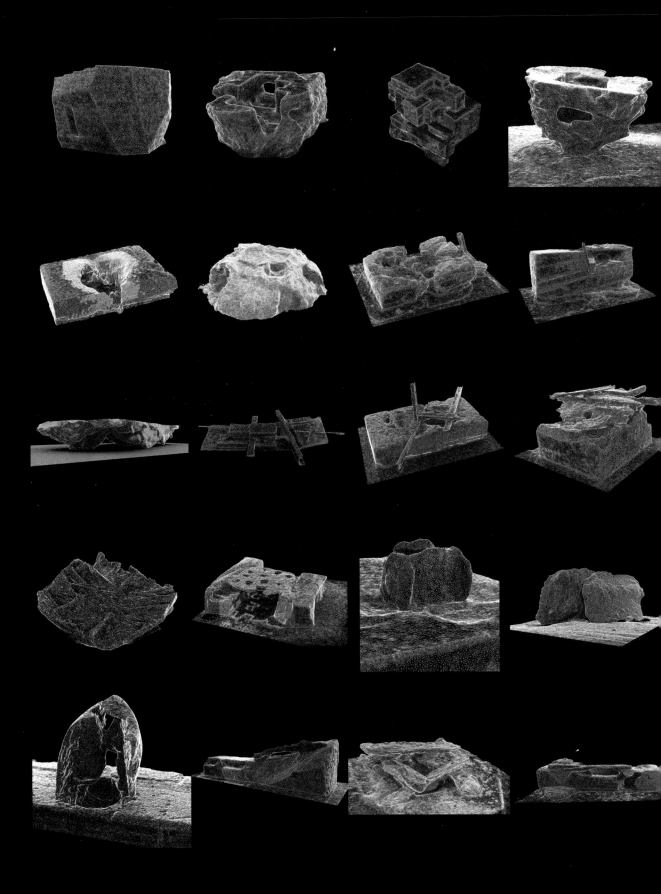

Once architectural concepts are conceived while being materialized, the transfer from matter to data occurs via 3D scanning technologies which ensure the most accurate translation. Engineering follows.

From these 30 potential projects, three have already been built: Beartooth Portal, Inverted Portal and Domo. The three of them are equal parts shelter and performance space. Others await their opportunity to exist.

建築のコンセプトが考案され、具現化されると、もっとも精密な3Dスキャニング技術を用いて、その物質（模型）を3Dデータに変換する。続いて構造設計が行われる。

30の実現を目指すプロジェクトのうち、すでに「ベアトゥース・ポータル」、「インバーテッド・ポータル」、「ドーモ」の3つは建設されている。これら3つは、雨風から守るシェルターとしての役割とパフォーマンススペースを兼ねている。ほかのプロジェクトは、実現される機会を待っている。

MASTERPLAN
Constellation

マスタープラン
星座

3 RETICULA
(Unbuilt)

レティクラ
(アンビルト)

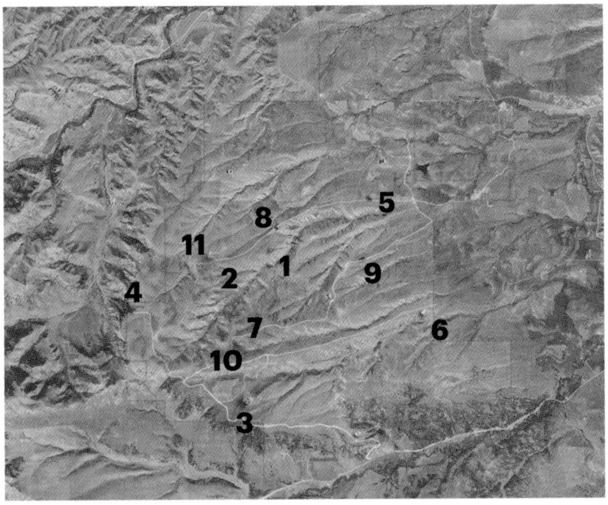

1 BALDACCHINO
(Unbuilt)

バルダッキーノ
(アンビルト)

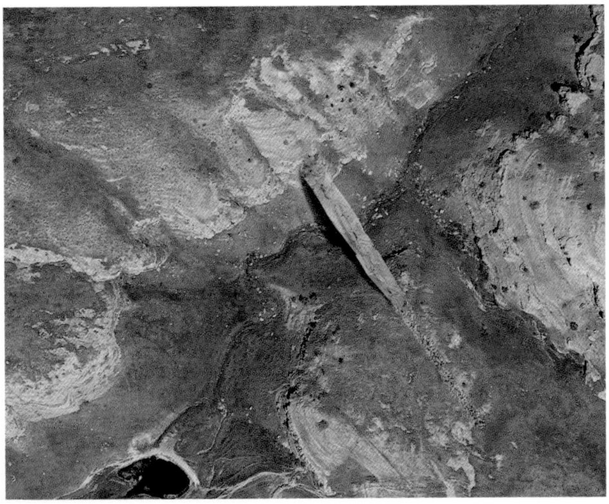

4 MIDNIGHT ROSTRA
(Unbuilt)

ミッドナイト・ロストラ
(アンビルト)

2 PONTE
(Unbuilt)

ポンテ
(アンビルト)

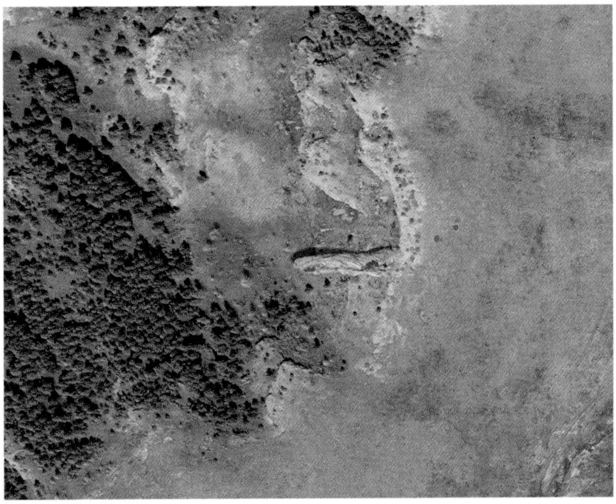

5 FIRST STONE
(Unbuilt)

ファースト・ストーン
(アンビルト)

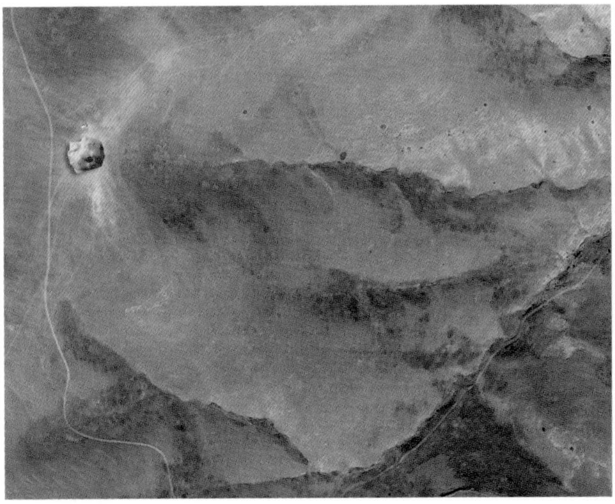

6 AKADEMIA アカデミア
(Unbuilt) (アンビルト)

7 FONTANA フォンタナ
(Unbuilt) (アンビルト)

8 BEARTOOTH PORTAL ベアトゥース・ポータル
(Built) (竣工)

9 INVERTED PORTAL インバーテッド・ポータル
(Built) (竣工)

10 DOMO ドーモ
(Built) (竣工)

11 TABULA タブラ
(Unbuilt) (アンビルト)

BEARTOOTH PORTAL ベアトゥース・ポータル（ベアトゥース山脈への門）

Site Preparation
敷地造成

Molding Phase
成形

Reinforcing Phase
鉄筋配置

0   10 m

The land serves as the natural and most economical formwork to cast these structures. It is stirred and molded, making the bed that will bring to life architectures as pieces of landscape. On the sites where they will sit, they first lay down, in gas state, then liquid and finally solid.

大地は、これらの構造体の打設のための自然な、もっとも経済的な型枠としての役割を果たす。それは攪拌され、成形され、ランドスケープの断片になる建築に命を吹き込む土台になる。将来の居場所として定められた敷地に、それらは最初に気体、その後、液体、最終的に固体となって横たわる。

They rest covered for 28 days, until they acquire full mechanical strength in full form. It is then that they get unearthed, picked, and lifted to their final location.

それらは完全な力学的強度と形を得るまで、28日間養生される。その後、掘り出され、持ち上げられて、最終的な位置に据えられる。

Casting Phase
コンクリート打設

Tilting Phase
傾転作業

0   10 m

INVERTED PORTAL インバーテッド・ポータル （裏返された門）

Reinforcement Phase

鉄筋工事

0.44 [1' 5 1/2"]

Ø 12/ 0.20
[#4 @ 8" max. both ways]

Ø 12/ 0.20
[#4 @ 8" max. both ways]

0.79 [2' 7"]

0.95 [3' 1 1/2"]

Ø 16/ 0.20
[#5 @ 8" max. both ways]

Ø 12/ 0.20
[#4 @ 8" max. both ways]

Ø 16/ 0.20
[#5 @ 8" max. both ways]

1.13 [3' 8 1/2"]

10.63 [34' 10 1/2"]

1.45 [4' 9"]

0.60 [1' 11 1/2"]

12.83 [42' 1"]

1.74 [5' 8 3/4"]

Ø 12/ 0.20
[#4 @ 8" max. both ways]

1.26 [4' 1 1/2"]

0.96 [3' 1 1/2"]

1.07 [3' 6"]

1.24 [4' 1"]

Ø 12/ 0.20 [#4 @ 8" max. both ways]

Structural Plan

構造平面図

0   5 m

Casting Phase
コンクリート打設工事

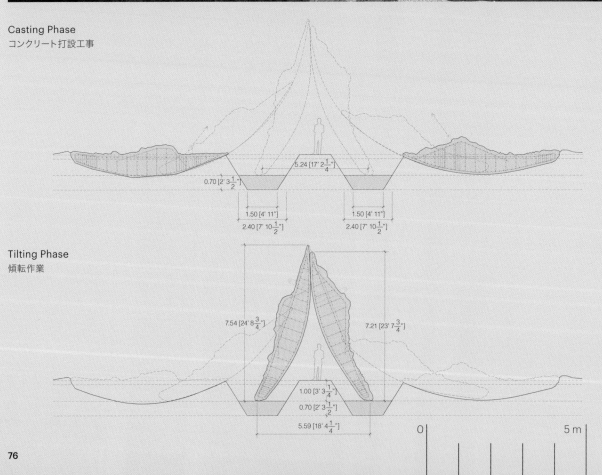

5.24 [17' 2 1/4"]

0.70 [2' 3 1/2"]

1.50 [4' 11"]　　1.50 [4' 11"]

2.40 [7' 10 1/2"]　　2.40 [7' 10 1/2"]

Tilting Phase
傾転作業

7.54 [24' 8 3/4"]　　7.21 [23' 7 3/4"]

1.00 [3' 3 1/4"]

0.70 [2' 3 1/2"]

5.59 [18' 4 1/4"]

0　　　　　　5 m

DOMO ドーモ（丸屋根）

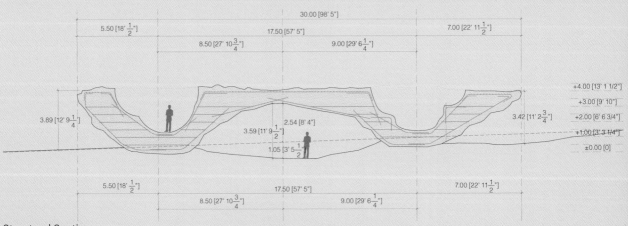

Structural Section
構造断面図

30.00 [98' 5"]

5.50 [18' $\frac{1}{2}$"]   17.50 [57' 5"]   7.00 [22' 11$\frac{1}{2}$"]

8.50 [27' 10$\frac{3}{4}$"]   9.00 [29' 6$\frac{1}{4}$"]

3.89 [12' 9$\frac{1}{4}$"]

2.54 [8' 4"]

3.59 [11' 9$\frac{1}{2}$"]

1.05 [3' 5$\frac{1}{2}$"]

3.42 [11' 2$\frac{3}{4}$"]

+4.00 [13' 1 1/2"]
+3.00 [9' 10"]
+2.00 [6' 6 3/4"]
+1.00 [3' 3 1/4"]
±0.00 [0]

5.50 [18' $\frac{1}{2}$"]   17.50 [57' 5"]   7.00 [22' 11$\frac{1}{2}$"]

8.50 [27' 10$\frac{3}{4}$"]   9.00 [29' 6$\frac{1}{4}$"]

0   15 m

Structures of Landscape enable habitation without exploitation and intimate relationships with the environment. They resonate with the immensity, the roughness, the silence and the magical loneliness of the place amplifying its values, and situate our actions in an ambiguous position between nature, architecture and art; they can be one and all, or a completely different category that only makes sense where it was born.

「ランドスケープの構造体」は、自然を搾取しない居住、そして環境との親密な関係を可能にする。それらは、この場所の巨大さ、荒々しさ、静寂、魔法のような孤独と響き合い、その価値を増幅させ、ランドスケープの構造体をつくるという私たちの行動を、自然、建築、芸術の間に曖昧に位置付ける。自然、建築、芸術はひとつですべてと呼べるものかもしれないし、この作品が生まれるこの場所でしか意味をなさないようなそれぞれにまったく異なる分野だとも言える。

TABULA タブラ（台）

Complementing Beartooth Portal, Inverted Portal and Domo, other structures are further developed to articulate the future growth of the art center. In the same spirit, they are conceived as raw architecture that is expressive and acoustically precise. Construction methodologies are designed in consonance with the architectural ideas, blending the technologically primitive with the highly advanced.

ティペット・ライズ・アート・センターの今後の成長を確かなものにするために、「ベアトゥース・ポータル」、「インバーテッド・ポータル」、「ドーモ」を補完するほかの構造物の計画もさらに進められている。それらは同じように表現豊かで、精密な音響を備えつつも、自然のままの建築として考案される。建築の考え方に基づき、原始的な技術と高度な技術を合わせた施工方法が開発される。

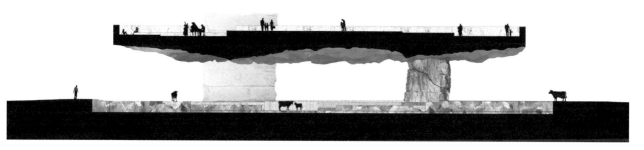

Section
断面図

Like an ancient Greek temple, Tabula sits on a hill, overlooking the surrounding landscape, building a performance stage for larger audiences and spectacles. Its broken ceiling recreates the space of the mountains and enables a monumental acoustic immersion.

「タブラ」は、古代ギリシャの神殿のように周囲の風景を見渡せる丘の上に置かれ、大勢の観客と公演のための舞台を構築する。断片化された天井は周囲の山々の空間を再現し、壮大な音の世界に没入させてくれる。

0   20 m

BALDACCHINO バルダッキーノ （キャノピー）

Baldacchino builds an
open room on the land,
a site for meditation and
artistic expression as well
as a stop along the way.

「バルダッキーノ」は、瞑想と
芸術表現の場として、または
道中の休憩所として、大地の
上に開けた空間を構築する。

0　　　　　　　　　　10 m

FIRST STONE ファースト・ストーン

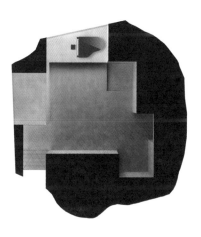

First Stone encloses
an auditorium space,
fully protected from the
elements and isolated
from the views; it is a
place to disconnect
from the immensity of
the landscape by hiding
inside a piece of it.

「ファースト・ストーン」 は、
オーディトリアムの空間を内
包し、風雨から守り、眺望を
遮る。風景の断片のなかに隠
れて、風景の巨大さから自分
を切り離すための場所だ。

0   10 m

FONTANA フォンタナ （泉）

Fontana connects with existing flows on the site, activating and making them visible. It collects underground water, rainwater and snow, filtering and separating them to make them available for visitors and animals alike.

「フォンタナ」（泉）は、敷地内にある流れとつながり、それらに活気を与え、可視化する。地下水、雨水や雪を集め、ろ過して分離し、訪問者や動物たちが利用できるようにする。

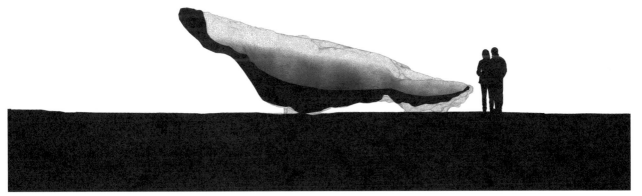

0   5 m

PONTE ポンテ（橋）

Ponte connects two
disconnected parts
of the ranch, crossing
across Murphy Canyon
and building a new path
for visitors to explore
the land.

「ポンテ」（橋）は、牧場の
ふたつの離れている部分を
つなぎ、マーフィー・キャニオン
を横断して、訪問者が大地を
探索するための新しい道を
構築する。

MIDNIGHT ROSTRA ミッドナイト・ロストラ （真夜中の演壇）

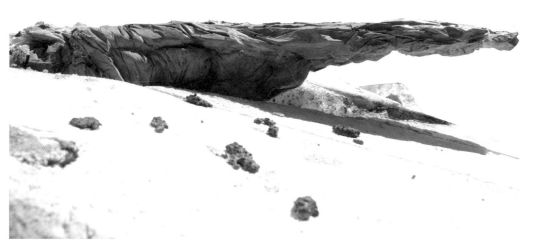

Midnight Rostra cantilevers over Midnight Canyon, providing a privileged viewing platform from which to experience the magnificence of nature.

「ミッドナイト・ロストラ」（真夜中の演壇）は、ミッドナイト・キャニオンの上に張り出し、壮大な自然を経験できる特別な展望台を構築する。

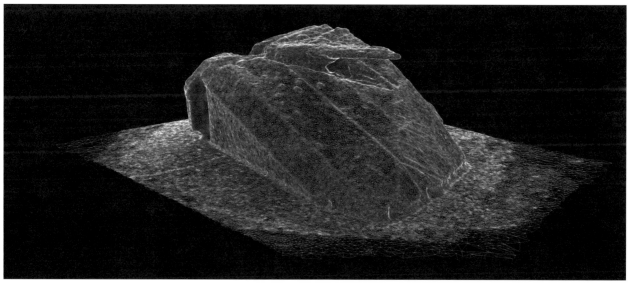

0

10 m

AKADEMIA アカデミア

Akademia is an altar for discussion and debate among visitors and residents. Created from an explosion of matter, it welcomes vibrant ideas and interactions.

「アカデミア」は訪問者と住民の間で議論をするための場所だ。物質の爆発から生まれた「アカデミア」は、刺激的なアイディアや交流を喜んで受け入れる。

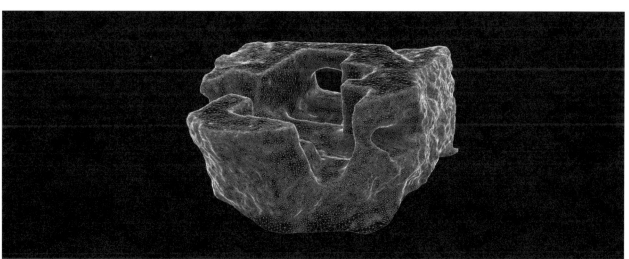

0   10 m

Developing Structures of Landscape, new typologies emerge while old ones get reinterpreted in relation to the Earth. We continue our explorations through new projects and new places, exploiting the material, structural and spatial potentialities of our previous findings.

Grids, towers and bridges are revisited in the next pages, bringing our research closer to urban grounds and forms.

「ランドスケープの構造体」の設計を進めるなかで、古いタイポロジーが大地との関係において再解釈されると同時に、新しいタイポロジーが現れる。これまでに見いだした材料、構造、空間の潜在的な可能性を活用しながら、新しいプロジェクトや新しい場所を通して探求を続ける。

次のページからは、グリッド、塔、橋を再訪する。私たちの研究は、都市の大地、都市の形へと近づいていく。

RETICULA

レティクラ

for Governors Island, New York, New York, USA 2017

米国、ニューヨーク州、ニューヨーク、ガバナーズ・アイランド

99

Reticula takes the urban grid, one of the most artificial and ubiquitous instruments used to plan the land, and develops an architecture that questions its efficiencies. Departing from the orthogonal intersection of lines that define quadrants, it deforms this framework to adapt; adapt to the topography, adapt to spaces and programs, and adapt to the character of the context that it organizes. It deforms and while doing so, subverts the idea of the grid, so that quadrants are no longer parcels but voids filled with air and views.

As a metaphor of the urban grid, there is no better place to test this concept than in New York City. NY Reticula rests on Governors' Island Park, a privileged site south of Manhattan, a piece of landscape with outstanding environmental qualities that can be reached by ferry from both Manhattan and Brooklyn's closest shores. The island, which contains a number of historic buildings in the process of restoration, has also become home to enticing landscape interventions looking to preserve and enhance the unique characteristics of the site while guiding the development. In this evolving ecosystem, NY Reticula situates itself as a continuation of the recently completed park, exciting its topography, settling in between hills, lawns, trees, paths, water... and expanding the existing cultural, artistic and recreational functions through its sheltering structure.

Site Plan
配置図

Participating in a seamless experience of the island, visitors smoothly transition from the meandering paths of the park to the covered outdoor spaces of Reticula, to its interior, and to the roof where panoramic views of Governors Island, Manhattan, Brooklyn, Staten Island and New Jersey, can be enjoyed.

0   5000 m

「レティクラ」では、土地を計画する上でもっとも人工的でユビキタスな手段のひとつである都市のグリッドに着目し、その効果を問う建築を考案する。それは平面を分割し細分化する、直交する直線から出発するが、さまざまな要因に適応するために、この枠組みは変形し、土地の地形に適応し、空間やプログラムに適応し、それ自身がつくり出すコンテクストの特性に適応する。それは変形すると同時にグリッドの概念を覆し、分割された平面はもはやただの小区画ではなく、景色を見渡せる空気に満たされたヴォイドになる。

都市のグリッドのメタファーとしてのこのコンセプトを試すのに、ニューヨークはもっともふさわしい場所だろう。ニューヨークの「レティクラ」は、マンハッタンの南に位置するガバナーズ・アイランド・パークにあり、マンハッタンとブルックリンのもっとも近い岸からフェリーで行くことができる、すばらしい環境に恵まれた特別な景観の一角をなす。修復中の歴史的建造物が数多く存在するこの島では、開発が進められる一方で、この場所の独自の特徴を維持し、さらに向上させることを目的とした、魅力的なランドスケープの介入が行われている。この進化する生態系のなかで、ニューヨークの「レティクラ」は、最近完成した公園の延長として自らを位置付け、地形に作用し、丘、芝生、樹木、道、水などの間に居場所を定めて、そこを護る構造体としての役割を果たすことで、既存の文化・芸術・レクリエーションの機能をさらに広げている。

Plan +5.00 m
平面図 +5.00 m

訪問者は島をシームレスに経験し、公園の曲がりくねった小道から「レティクラ」の屋根付きの屋外スペース、内部空間、そしてガバナーズ・アイランド、マンハッタン、ブルックリン、スタテン・アイランド、ニュージャージーのパノラマの眺望が楽しめる屋上へと滑らかに移行する。

0   150 m

As if extracted from the island's bedrock, NY Reticula brings together architecture and nature in a way that resounds with the geology of the site. Granite rocks from the island's old seawall that were used to build the park are used here again to conglomerate the cyclopean concrete that will support the spaces of Reticula.

島の岩盤から抜き取られたかのように、ニューヨークの「レティクラ」は敷地の地質と響き合うようなかたちで、建築と自然を融合している。公園の建設に使われた、島の古い防波堤から採取される花崗岩の岩石は、ここでは「レティクラ」の空間を支持する巨石コンクリートの粗骨材として、再利用されている。

Sections
断面図

Elevations
立面図

0

100 m

Plan
平面図

Walking inside Reticula feels like inhabiting the core of a giant rock. Spaces interlock as if carved by water, leaving the eroded mass to serve as protective structure.

「レティクラ」の中を歩くと、まるで巨大な岩の真ん中に住んでいるような感覚を覚える。水によって彫り込まれたかのように空間が絡み合い、侵食された岩の塊が、その場所を護る構造体としての役割を果たす。

0   50 m

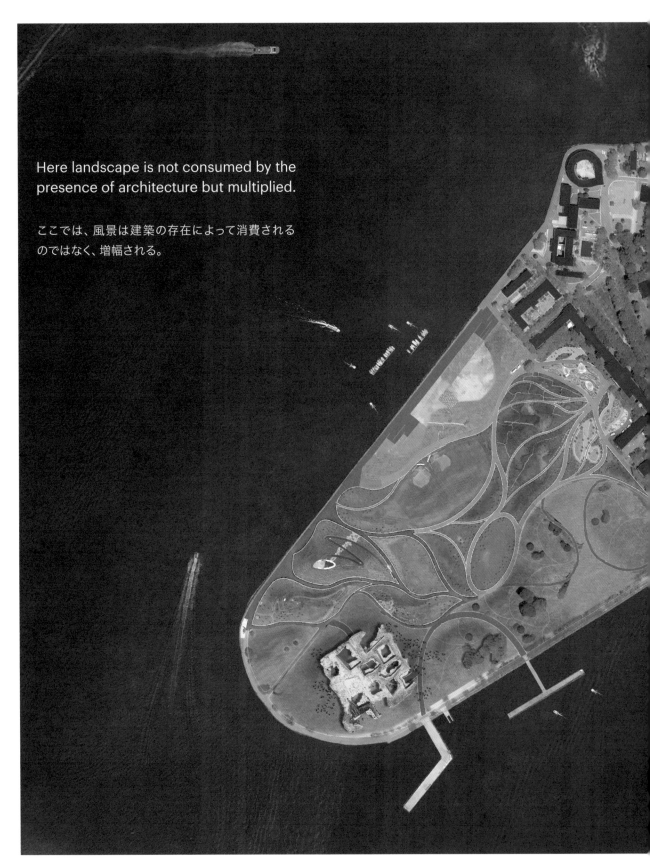

Here landscape is not consumed by the
presence of architecture but multiplied.

ここでは、風景は建築の存在によって消費される
のではなく、増幅される。

0

500 m

From our experiences so far, we have learned about the magnetic relationship between people and the spaces of nature, the spaces that incarnate nature, that enact nature or that simply refer to it in relevant ways. Because of their roughness, their wildness, their low resolution, their continuous transformation, their connection with the essential and disconnection with urban environments, their lack of determinacy that liberates the spirit and excites the imagination... we are inherently attracted to such spaces, structures, and images.

Now we feel compelled to rethink about other well-known typology, the tower!, in our quest for new "natures", for an architecture of the Earth that invades some of the spaces reserved for monotonous industrialized structures, where the natural and the artificial blur, and where architecture is allowed to refer to the space of the mountains, the canyons, the cliffs and the caves.

これまでの経験から、私たちは、人と自然の空間、自然を具現化する空間、自然を演じる空間、あるいは単純に適切な方法で自然を参照した空間の、互いに引き付け合う関係性について学んできた。それらの荒々しさ、果てしない広がり、解像度の低さ、絶え間ない変化、本質的なものとのつながり、都市環境との断絶、精神を解放し想像力をかき立てる確定性の欠如……、私たちは、そのような空間、構造、イメージに本質的に魅かれている。

さて、私たちは新しい「自然」、そして単調な産業化された構築物のために確保された空間の一部に忍び込む「地球の建築」——自然と人工が曖昧になり、山、峡谷、崖、洞窟などの空間をよりどころとする建築——を探し求めるなかで、ほかのよく知られたタイポロジー、たとえば塔（!）を再考したいという思いに駆られている。

TOWERS OF LANDSCAPE

ランドスケープの塔

2017

While towers are typically designed for efficiency and repetition, producing identical stacks of spaces that maximize the use of a given plot of land, this investigation understands the building as part of the land; as a hill, or a mountain that is eroded, carved, cut or exploded to enable novel spatialities and programs, and to provide experiences yet unknown.

一般的に塔は効率性と反復性を旨として設計され、与えられた土地を最大限利用するために、同じ空間を
積み重ねた建築を生み出すが、この研究では、新しい空間性やプログラムを実現するために、この建築を
大地の一部として、そして侵食されたり、彫り込まれたり、切断されたり、爆破されたりする丘や山として
解釈する。

Construction processes are crafted according to the spatial and material ideas behind each work. The resulting spaces and architectures appear as a consequence of the actions placed on matter. They are powerful and unique.

それぞれの作品の背景にある空間的・物質的な考えに従って、施工プロセスが編み出される。物質に対して
なされた行為の結果として、空間と建築が現れる。それらは力強く、唯一無二のものだ。

EXCAVATED TOWER 掘り込まれた塔

LAYERED TOWER 積層する塔

3D GRID TOWER 3Dグリッドの塔

MELTED TOWER 溶解する塔

Towers of Landscape were created without a site. These blocks of artificial landscape are made to fit generic urban grids, substituting private floors for public grounds.

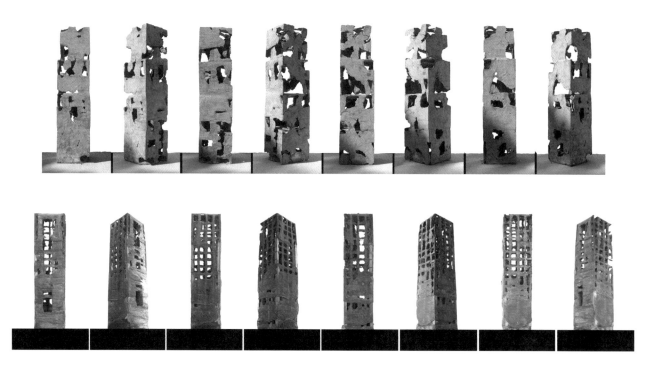

「ランドスケープの塔」は、敷地を想定せずに考案された。これらの人工的なランドスケープの塊は、一般的な
都市のグリッドに合わせてつくられており、個人が所有する床面ではなく、公共の地盤面として機能する。

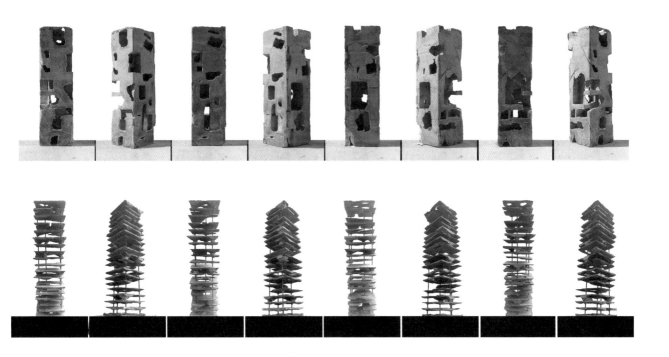

Our research on hybrid typologies progresses merging infrastructure with landscape, to create infrastructural works that become extensions of the landscape, or artificial landscapes which perform as infrastructures. Petrified River research reimagines bridges as rivers, rivers as rocks, and rocks as bridges. Projects like Petrified River for Cooper Hewitt Smithsonian Design Museum or Petrified River for the Irish National War Memorial Gardens, illustrate potential applications of this investigation.

私たちは、インフラとランドスケープを融合させ、ランドスケープの延長としてのインフラ、インフラとして機能するランドスケープをつくり出すために、ハイブリッドなタイポロジーの研究を進めている。「石化した川」の研究では、橋を川として、川を岩として、岩を橋として再考する。クーパー・ヒューイット国立デザイン博物館で展示された「石化した川」や、アイルランド国立戦争記念碑庭園内コンペティション案の「石化した川」などのプロジェクトでは、この研究の応用の可能性を例示している。

PETRIFIED RIVER

ペトリファイド・リバー（石化した川）

2017

121

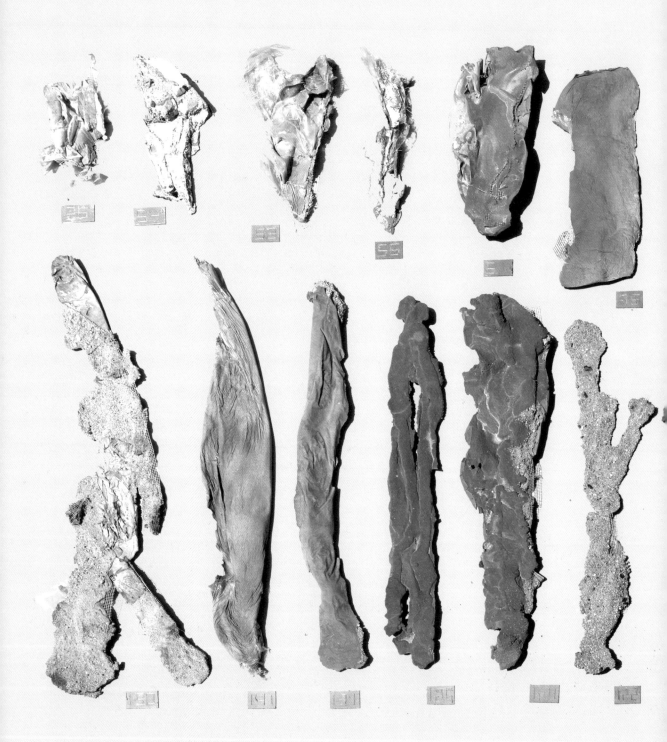

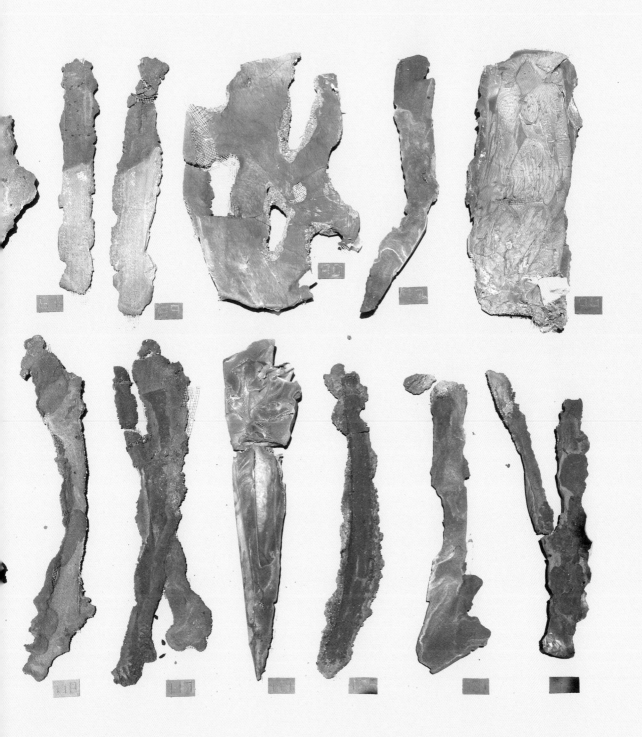

Installation at Cooper Hewitt Smithsonian Design Museum, New York, New York, USA 2019

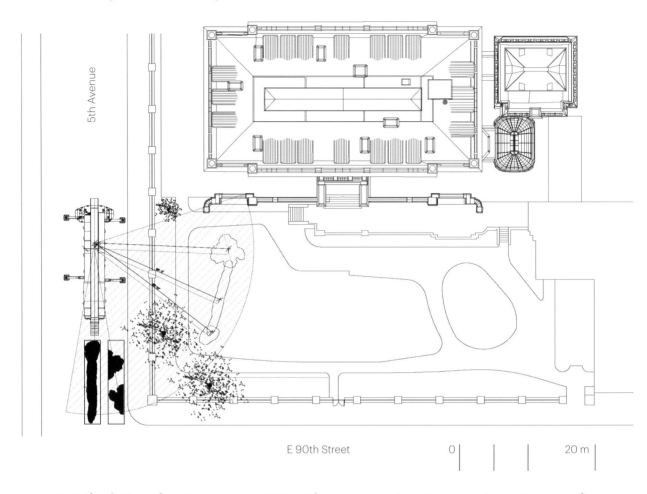

5th Avenue

E 90th Street

0   20 m

Petrified River for Cooper Hewitt Smithsonian Design Museum is a site-specific installation that occupied the museum's garden during the 2019 Design Triennial exhibition, *Nature*. To materialize this investigation in a museum context, in New York City, and right across from Central Park, we look at the history of the city. The transformation process of Manhattan from wild nature to urbanized flattened land has involved enormous efforts and a massive exploitation of the land digging, leveling, exploding, reclaiming, filling and the consequential disappearance of some of its natural geographical features.

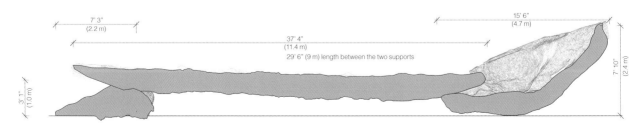

7' 3"
(2.2 m)

15' 6"
(4.7 m)

37' 4"
(11.4 m)
29' 6" (9 m) length between the two supports

7' 10"
(2.4 m)

3' 1"
(1.0 m)

0   5 m

米国、ニューヨーク州、ニューヨーク、クーパー・ヒューイット国立デザイン博物館での展示

The proposal, a hill, a river and a pond—made of concrete—serves as a petrified metaphor of the rich landscape that Manhattan once was, when it was still known as Mannahatta or "island of many hills". It is meant to embody the intriguing collision between the infrastructural, the industrial, the artistic, the geological... the difficult balance between the artificial and the natural. A dilemma clearly showcased right across the street, in Central Park, a completely artificial landscape that New Yorkers cherish as their most symbolic piece of nature.

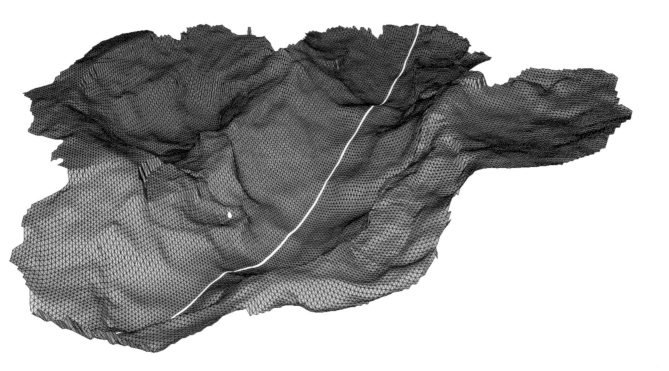

クーパー・ヒューイット国立デザイン博物館で展示された「石化した川」は、2019年のデザイン・トリエンナーレ展「Nature」の期間中、博物館の庭園に設置されたサイト・スペシフィックのインスタレーションだ。ニューヨークのセントラルパークの真向かいにある博物館という環境でこの研究をかたちにするために、私たちはこの街の歴史を調べた。マンハッタンが手つかずの自然から都市化された平坦な土地へ変貌する過程では、膨大な労力をかけて土地の大規模な開発（掘削、整地、爆破、埋立、埋戻し）が行われ、その結果、自然の地理的特徴の一部が消滅してしまった。

私たちが提案するコンクリートでできた丘、川、池は、かつて「Mannahatta」（多くの丘の島）として知られていたマンハッタンにあった豊かなランドスケープの石化されたメタファーとしての役割を果たす。この作品は、インフラ、産業、芸術、地質を魅力的なかたちで衝突させ、人工と自然の難しいバランスを実現させることを意図している。通りの向かい側にあるセントラルパーク、ニューヨーカーがもっとも象徴的な自然の断片として大事にしている完全に人工的なランドスケープが、このジレンマを明確に表している。

POND Fabrication　池の製作

Given the project requirements -a removable installation in the center of a busy city-, we attempt a new practical feat: to pre-fabricate this artificial landscape. We build it in Ensamble Fabrica, in Madrid.

人通りの多い街の中心部に撤去可能なインスタレーションを設置するというプロジェクトの要件を考慮して、私たちはこの人工的なランドスケープを組立工法で製作するという斬新で実践的な離れ業を試みた。マドリッドのアンサンブル・ファブリカで製作した。

Design and Engineering Phase
設計とエンジニアリング工程

Prefabrication Phase
プレファブリケーション工程

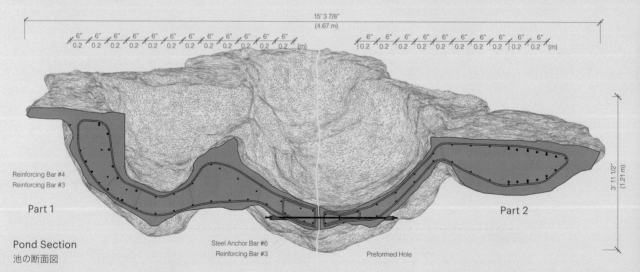

15' 3 7/8"
(4.67 m)

6" 6" 6" 6" 6" 6" 6" 6" 6" 6" 6" 6"
0.2 0.2 0.2 0.2 0.2 0.2 0.2 0.2 0.2 0.2 0.2 0.2 (m)

6" 6" 6" 6" 6" 6" 6" 6" 6" 6"
0.2 0.2 0.2 0.2 0.2 0.2 0.2 0.2 0.2 0.2 (m)

3' 11 1/2"
(1.21 m)

Reinforcing Bar #4
Reinforcing Bar #3

Part 1

Part 2

Pond Section
池の断面図

Steel Anchor Bar #6
Reinforcing Bar #3

Preformed Hole

0　　　　　　　　　1 m

RIVER Fabrication　川の製作

0.0000E0 -0.3750E0 -0.7500E0 -1.1250E0 -1.5000E0 -1.8750E0 -2.2500E0 -2.6250E0 -3.0000E0 -3.3750E0 -3.7500E0 -4.1250E0 -4.5000E0 -4.8750E0 -5.2500E0 -5.6250E0 -6.0000E0 -6.3750E0 -6.7500E0 -7.1250E0 -7.5000E0 -7.8750E0 -8.2500E0 -8.6250E0 -9.0000E0 -9.3750E0 -9.7500E0 -1.0125E1 -1.0500E1 -1.0875E1 -1.1250E1 -1.1625E1 -1.2000E1 -1.2375E1 -1.2750E1 -1.3125E1 -1.3500E1 -1.3875E1 -1.4250E1 -1.4625E1 -1.5000E1 -3.2435E5

Structural Analysis
構造解析

0　　　　　　　　3 m

Shipping and Assembly　運送と組立

Once casted and cured, Hill, River and Pond are placed in two shipping containers to be transported across the Atlantic and delivered to their initial destination.

丘、川、池は、打設と養生の完了後、大西洋の向こうの最初の目的地に向けて発送するために、ふたつのコンテナに入れられる。

They are installed overnight, on a Saturday, during the very few quiet hours that the 5th Avenue in New York City enjoys. They will rest on the museum's lawn for a few months, and will then travel west, leaving no physical trace of their stay.

土曜日の夜、それらはニューヨーク五番街が静寂に包まれる数時間の間に設置される。それらは数か月の間、博物館の芝生の上で休息した後、西へと旅立つ。何も痕跡を残さずに。

Container Layout
コンテナ内の配置

40' 0"
(12.2 m)
39' 6"
(12.0 m)

40' 0"
(12.2 m)
39' 6"
(12.0 m)

7' 7"
(2.3 m)
8' 0"
(2.4 m)

7' 7"
(2.3 m)
8' 0"
(2.4 m)

Plan 平面図

40' 0"
(12.2 m)
39' 6"
(12.0 m)

40' 0"
(12.2 m)
39' 6"
(12.0 m)

7' 7"
(2.3 m)
8' 0"
(2.4 m)

7' 7"
(2.3 m)
8' 0"
(2.4 m)

Section 断面図

Container 1 River, Hill
コンテナ 1 川、丘

Container 2 Pond Part 1, Pond Part 2
コンテナ 2 池 パート1、池 パート2

0   10 m

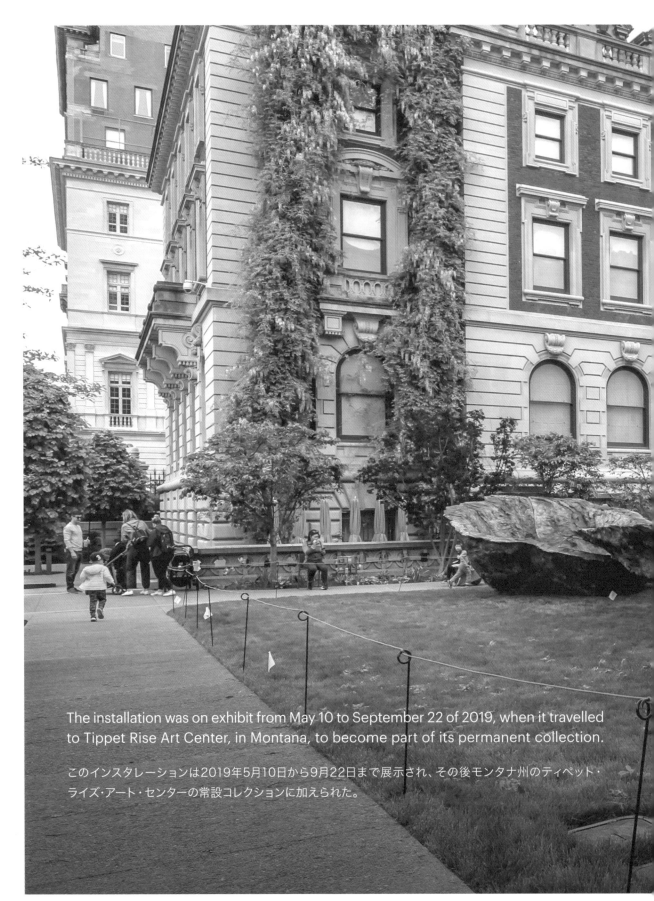

The installation was on exhibit from May 10 to September 22 of 2019, when it travelled to Tippet Rise Art Center, in Montana, to become part of its permanent collection.

このインスタレーションは2019年5月10日から9月22日まで展示され、その後モンタナ州のティペット・ライズ・アート・センターの常設コレクションに加えられた。

Proposal for the Commemorative Bridge at INWMG in Islandbridge, Dublin, Ireland 2019

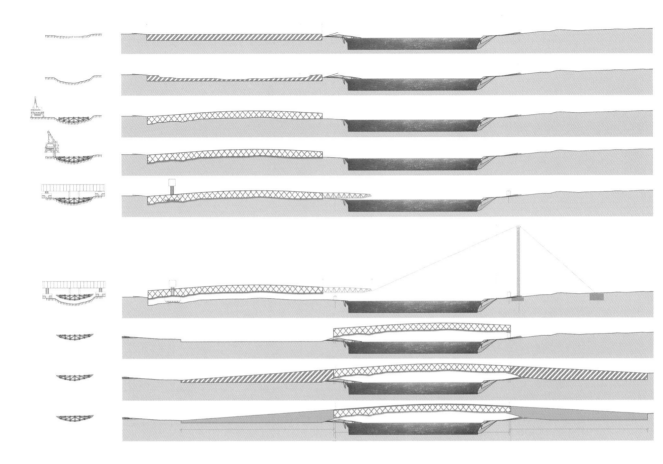

From installation to civil work, our proposal for the Commemorative Bridge at the Irish National War Memorial Gardens in Islandbridge, Dublin, creates a bridge as an extension of the park, building a strong connection between both banks of River Liffey. As part of our research on Petrified Rivers, the project combines the efficiency of an engineering work with the material and formal qualities of a landscape.

The bridge has an organic plan, with a total length of 140 m and variable width that ranges from 6 to 10 m. Concrete becomes the main visible material, providing a resistant crust that requires reduced maintenance. The expressive nature of the material is exploited to achieve a myriad of colors and textures that will help distinguish different speeds and functions of the bridge: the pavement is smoother at the center line of the bridge to best serve cycling lanes, and becomes rougher towards the sides increasing the resistance to slipping on pedestrian areas and integrating vegetation on its irregular edges.

0   50 m

アイルランド、ダブリン、アイランドブリッジ、アイルランド国立戦争記念碑庭園内コンペティション応募案

「石化した川」は仮設インスタレーションから土木建造物へ。ダブリンのアイランドブリッジにあるアイルランド国立戦争記念碑庭園内のコンペティション応募案は、公園の延長としての橋を架け、リフィー川の両岸を強く結びつけることを意図している。「石化した川」の研究の一環として、このプロジェクトは、エンジニアリングの効率性とランドスケープの物質や形態の性質を融合している。

ブリッジは、全長140m、幅は6mから10mまで変化する有機的な平面で構成される。表に見える主な材料としてコンクリートを用いて、メンテナンスをあまり必要としない耐久性のある外皮をつくり出す。利用者のさまざまな移動速度や必要な機能に対応するため、コンクリートの表現性を利用してさまざまな色や材質感の工夫がなされている。舗装は、中心線に沿ったサイクリングレーンでは走行しやすいように滑らかに仕上げ、両側に向かって粗面に仕上げることで歩行者エリアの防滑性を高めており、不揃いな端部は植物と一体化している。

The bridge is a means of connection and a place of transit, but it is also a destination and a space for contemplation like the fountains, temples, monoliths, stairs and balustrades that articulate the Gardens.

橋は接続の手段であり、通過する場所であると同時に、この庭園を特徴付ける噴水、寺院、巨石、階段や手すりなどと同じように目的地であり、内省するための場所でもある。

Contemplating nature requires extracting information and processing it with sensibility. This information is perceived visually, but can also be heard, transpired, and most importantly, felt and incorporated into our memory. The emotions that we remember after visiting a space, a place or a landscape, give shape to what Le Corbusier called the "spirit of the place". Transforming this transcendent experience of memory into architecture involves a demanding process of translating abstract constructs into data, such as drawings, photographs, words or models, and this itinerary, from matter to data, allows us to preserve and enrich memory. As architects, we allow the impulses of our memory to activate the creative subconscious and excite the desire to create, to build, to interact with a place with its matter and with its spirit.

自然を考察するには、情報を抽出し、感覚的に処理する必要がある。この情報は視覚的に認識されるだけではなく、聴覚や嗅覚、触覚などすべての感覚で繊細に捉えられ、私たちの記憶に取り込まれることだ。私たちが空間、場所、ランドスケープを訪ねた後に思い出す感情は、ル・コルビュジエが「場所の精神」と呼んだものにかたちを与える。この超越的な記憶の経験を建築に変換するには、抽象的な構成要素を図面、写真、言葉や模型などのデータに変換するという難しい一連の作業をたどる必要がある。そして物質からデータへ変換するこの工程を通じて、私たちは記憶を保存し、さらに豊かにすることができる。建築家である私たちは、自分たちの記憶によって誘発されたクリエイティブな潜在意識を働かせて創造し、構築し、場所とその物質、その精神と対話したいという強い願いに動かされて行動する。

CULTIVATED STONES

耕された石

for Calderona House, Badajoz, Extremadura, Spain 2019

スペイン、エストレマドゥーラ州、バダホス、カルデローナの家

Visiting the hills of Calderona country estate in the heart of Extremadura surrounded by marshes, natural exuberance and silence, we find natural stone eruptions and provocative accidents of material beauty. We also discover forms traced by previous residents that later became vacant, ruined by time, suggestive, opposing the logic of the practical and embodying the beauty of the natural.

The departing point of our proposal is an intention to revive the accumulated popular knowledge that lies within the masonry stones of the found settlement, and to expose the new domestic spaces to the landscape from this platform of contemplation, respecting the memory of the place.

エストレマドゥーラ州の中心部に位置するカルデローナの湿地帯、豊かな自然、静寂に囲まれた丘を訪れ、自然石の爆発が引き起こした偶発的な物質の美を見いだす。そして、後に空き家になり、時間の経過とともに廃墟になった、過去の住人の残した痕跡をとどめる形も発見する。それらは示唆に富み、実用的な論理に反し、自然の美を体現している。

私たちの提案は、見いだされたすみかの石積みの内部に蓄積された人々の知識をよみがえらせて、場所の記憶を大切にしながら、新しい生活空間をこの内省の場所から風景に向けて開きたいという意図から始まっている。

View　外観

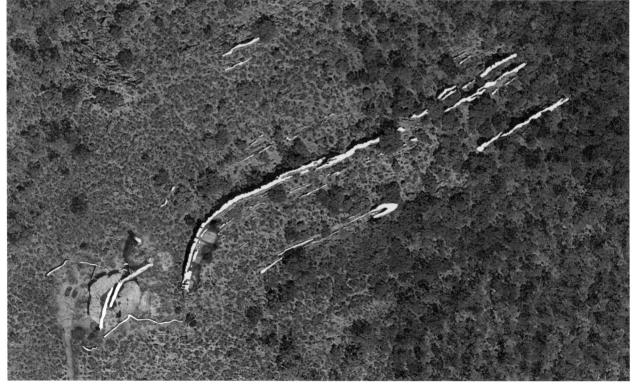

Plan　平面図

0 | | | | | 100 m

Over the stones of Calderona, we build other stones, cultivate them in the ground like we have learned to do, and free them from any architectural predetermination so that they can adapt to the orography, both materially and formally. New spaces appear as a result, which include shaded areas, sheltered rooms and framed views... We deliberately appropriate existing traces and add to them the structures of intuition that our sensitive memory induced after contemplating and interpreting the data of the landscape, of its matter, of its space and of its soul.

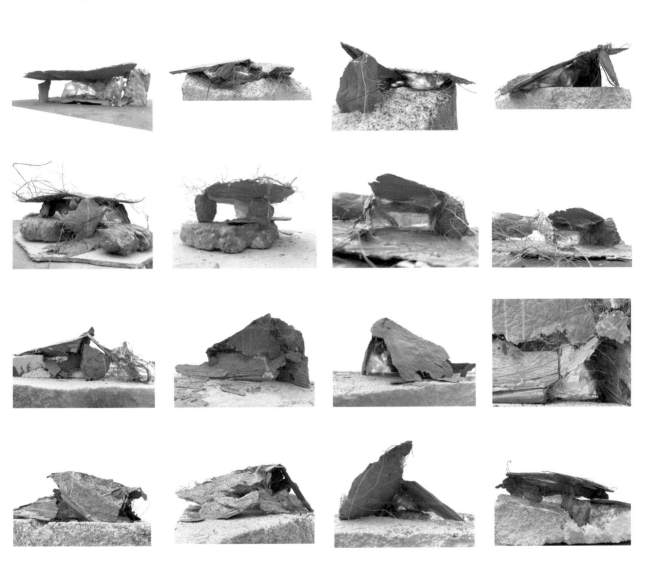

そしてカルデローナの石の上に別の石を構築し、私たちが習得したやり方でそれらを地面の中で育て、この山の地形に物質的にも形態的にも適応できるように、それらをあらゆる建築的な宿命から解放する。その結果、新しい空間、日陰になった場所、風雨から護られた部屋、切り取られた風景などが生まれる。私たちはそこにある痕跡を意図的に流用し、風景、その物質、その空間、その魂のデータを深く考察し、解釈した後、繊細な記憶に誘発され、直感に導かれてつくった構造体をそれらに加えていく。

From the Iberian to the Arabian Peninsula, from the rolling hills of Extremadura to the desert canyons of AlUla, a new extraordinary landscape excites our imagination. Here, like in Fishtail, Montana, we find a remote place far away from urbanization, awaiting to be stimulated and protected. This is a new mission that requires careful reading.

The AlUla region possesses a unique collection of landscapes. The inland desert plateau, the mountain ranges, and the wadi valleys offer extreme geological conditions and diverse habitats that closely coexist. On this barely urbanized land with its deep sandstone canyons, we develop Desert Rocks.

イベリア半島からアラビア半島、そしてエストレマドゥーラのなだらかな丘からアル・ウラーの砂漠に至るまで、新しい壮大な風景が私たちの想像力をかき立てる。モンタナ州フィッシュテイルと同様に、私たちはこの地に、都市化された場所から遠く離れた、新しい刺激と保護を待っている場所を見いだす。注意深い読み取りが求められる新しい任務だ。

アル・ウラーには、特徴的なランドスケープが集中している。内陸部の砂漠の高原、山脈、ワジ（涸れ川）の谷など、極端な地質条件と多様な動植物の生息環境が密接に共存している。ほとんど都市化されていない、深い砂岩の峡谷に位置するこの地で、私たちは「砂漠の岩」を考案した。

DESERT ROCKS

砂漠の岩

AlUla, Saudi Arabia 2020

サウジ・アラビア、アル・ウラー

145

MASTERPLAN
マスタープラン

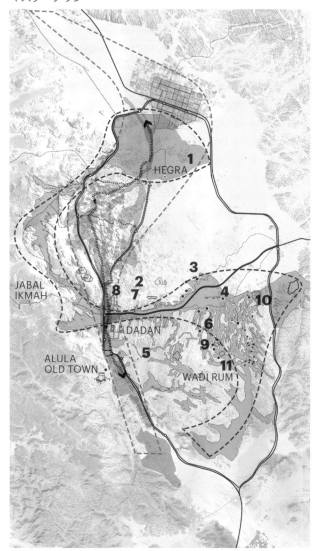

The project departs from identifying iconic rocks of AlUla and recognize their value as places. In harmony with the Nabatean monument of Madain Saleh, the pre-Arabic inscriptions of Jabal Ikmah and the many existing natural formations —Elephant Rock, Arch Rock, Hand Rock, etc.—, Desert Rocks introduce new destinations and energies in consonance with the ongoing efforts to develop the area.

このプロジェクトは、アル・ウラーの象徴的な岩を見つけて、それらの場所としての価値を認識することからはじまる。ナバテア文明のマダイン・サーレハ遺跡、古代アラビア語の碑文が刻まれたジャバル・イクマの岩、そしてエレファント・ロック、アーチ・ロック、ハンド・ロックなど数多く現存する自然の造形物と共存しながら、「砂漠の岩」は地域の発展のための継続的な取り組みと調和する新しい目的地やエネルギーを生み出す。

1 MADAIN SALEH
マダイン・サーレハ

2 ELEPHANT ROCK
エレファント・ロック

3 ARCH ROCK
アーチ・ロック

4 DUNE – ART CENTER
デューン／アート・センター

5 THERMA – ART BATHS
サーマ／アート・バス

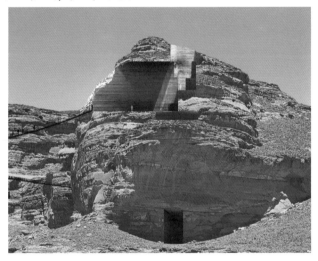

6 CANYON RESORT
キャニオン・リゾート

7 SLAB – VISITORS CENTER
スラブ／ビジターズ・センター

8 MENHIR – MUSEUM
メンヒル／ミュージアム

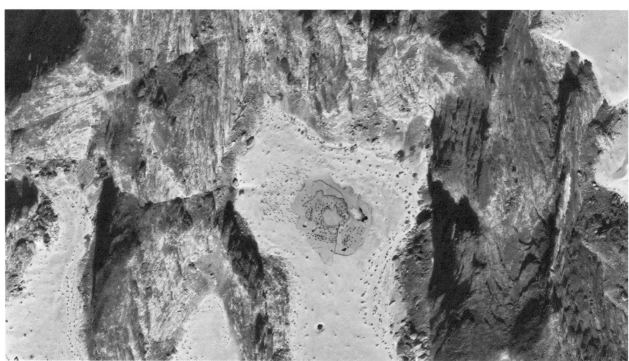

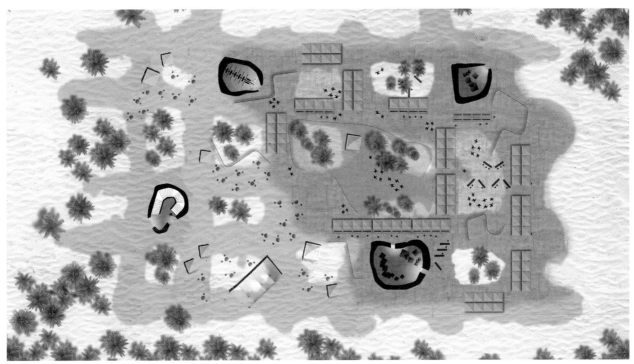

0 50 m

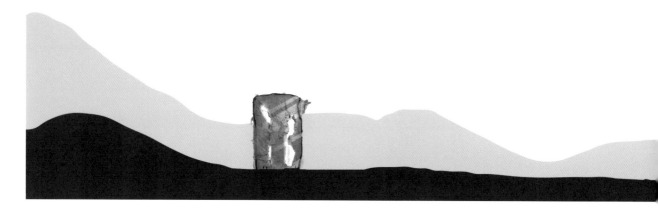

Old and new masses gravitate towards each other in balance in the universe of AlUla. Each one is unique, and occupies a dedicated space, filling the interstices of the landscape. All of them together configure a new layer, superimposed on the land. From these rocks, monumental, civic, hospitality and domestic spaces come into being, integrating art, architecture and landscape, and connecting human needs with artistic aspirations across times.

新旧のマッスは、アル・ウラーの宇宙の中で互いに引きつけ合い、引力に引かれながらバランスを保っている。それぞれが特徴的で、それ以外は何もない空間を占め、ランドスケープの隙間を埋めている。それらのすべてが一緒になって、大地に重ね合わされた新しいレイヤーを構成している。これらの岩から歴史的建造物、公共施設、宿泊施設、住宅などが立ち現れ、アート、建築、ランドスケープを統合し、時代を超えて人間のニーズと芸術的な野心を結び付けている。

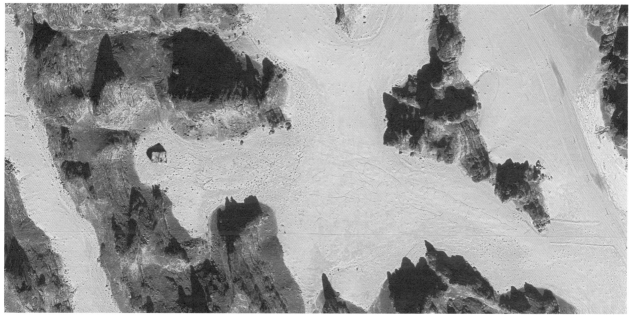

Our investigation is about to take a new leap, on the same site where we built The Truffle ten years ago, and with it, a decade of research and practice on how to cultivate a structure. Now we replace the ground for the air, the thick wall for the thin membrane and the rigid mold for the flexible one. We continue our architecture of action, our tranfers from matter to data to matter, our methods of indeterminacy and our aesthetics of imperfection. We do not have the next decade planned, but we see a long path ahead of us, full of intriguing discoveries from cultivating structures inside the earth to painting them in the air.

10年前に「トリュフ」を建設し、それを使って10年におよぶ構造物を育てる方法の研究と実践が行われている同じ敷地で、私たちの研究は新しい飛躍を遂げようとしている。今では私たちは地面の代わりに空気を、分厚い壁の代わりに薄い膜を、硬い型の代わりに柔らかい型を使っている。私たちは、行動の建築、物質からデータ、そしてまた物質への変換、不確定性を頼りにつくる方法、不完全性の美学を継続している。次の10年の計画は立てていないが、私たちの前には、たくさんの魅力的な発見につながる長い道がある。大地の中で構造物を育てることから、それらを空中に描くことまで。

THE TENT

テント

Costa da Morte, Spain 2020

スペイン、コスタ・ダ・モルテ

The Tent covers the space like a blanket. Its geometries adapt to the airy body that it delimits and embraces, without constraining it. Air and light flow through its openings, and the landscape sneaks in too, filling the cracks in the material. This architecture is hand-crafted, with hands that fold, connect, and dream up the structure and the space in unison. Starting with the model, which serves as a sketch and a miniature construction, we go on to data, scanning each movement and each detail, guided by intuition. After the designing comes the engineering, and then back to the designing. All of this happens over just five days, and then another five days to carry out the action in the rural environment. The construction is reminiscent of the design process in terms of its dynamic; the form has already been established, the structures calculated and the lines marked out.

「テント」は、空間をブランケットのように覆う。テントは空気で満たされた物体を束縛することなく、その境界を定めて包み込み、物体に合わせて形を変える。その開口部から空気と光が流れ込み、材料の隙間を埋めながら風景も忍び込んでくる。この建築は、折りたたみ、つなげると同時に構造物や空間は夢見る手によって成形される。スケッチやミニチュアの施工実験に用いる模型からはじまり、次に直感を頼りにすべての動きやディテールをスキャンしながら、データ化していく。設計の後はエンジニアリングに取り組み、その後また設計に戻る。このすべてがたった5日間で行われ、それから5日間かけてこの自然環境の中で私たちは行動する。施工は、試行錯誤しながら動的に進んでいったという意味では設計プロセスに似ていた。形態はすでに確立されており、構造は計算されており、線は引かれている。

The work gets underway by drawing the reinforcing bars in three dimensions; the measurements and proportions are checked and the orientation validated on site. When the lines have been validated, we start painting the structure, as if we were painting over a sketched-out canvas, adding material, texture and color in one unique, unrepeatable gesture. Layer by layer, its flexible folds get more rigid, its elastic membranes harden and its damp skin dries out. Layer by layer, an architecture materializes, one which is both fabric-like and rock-like, light and permanent, fluid and stony.

実空間に鉄筋で3次元の図面を描き、寸法とプロポーションを確認し、建物の正面の位置を決めることから作業がはじまる。線を確認したら、スケッチしたキャンバスの上に絵を描くように構造体を描き、一度しかできない、二度と繰り返せない動きで、材料、材質感、色を加えていく。層を重ねるごとにその柔らかい襞は硬くなり、弾力性のある膜は固まり、湿った表皮は乾いていく。層を重ねるごとに、建築が形になっていく。それは布のようでもあり岩のようでもあり、軽くて永続的で、流動的で石のようでもある。

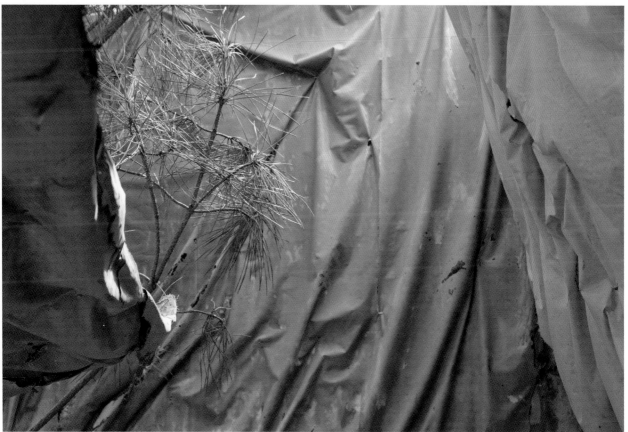

It rises from the ground and leans gently, as if it were meant to be a short-term structure, but its supports have taken root and they hold up a space that lies between the trees, looking out at the sea. It silently hopes to be taken in by nature, embraced and welcomed into the fold.

それは地面から立ち上がり、すぐに壊れてしまいそうな構造物のように緩やかに傾いているが、しっかり根を張った支柱で木々の間に横たわる空間を支えながら、海を眺めている。それは自然の一部になり、自然に抱かれ、その襞の中に受け入れてもらうことを静かに望んでいる。

As architects, our task usually involves creating new architectures and spaces, new layers of information and matter. We understand our actions as additive and we leave a clear imprint in the environment through them.

We want to finish this book with a silent action, with an act of creation that is not about adding but about observing, interpreting, and subtracting.

The reading of this place is not different from the ones we have done before. It is aimed at identifying potential and working with the land as a partner to give our most honest architectural response. In Ca'n Terra, the space was already created, and it was more beautiful than what we could have ever conceived. So why negate this fascinating discovery? Our act of creation becomes giving life to what was abandoned, dead.

建築家としての私たちの仕事は通常、新しい建築や空間、情報や物質の新しいレイヤーを創造することだ。私たちは自分たちの行動を加えていくことと捉えており、それらを通して環境に鮮明な跡を残す。

私たちはこの本を、寡黙な行為、すなわち、足し算ではなく、観察し、解釈し、引き算するという創造の行為で締めくくりたいと思う。

この場所の読み取り方は、以前にやっていたことと変わらない。それは、潜在的な可能性を見極め、パートナーとしてその土地に働きかけ、もっとも誠実な建築的対応をすることを目指している。「カン・テラ」では、空間はすでに出来上がっていた。そして、それは想像を絶するほど美しかった。このすばらしい発見を見過ごすことなどできない。私たちに課された創造行為は、見捨てられて死んだものに生命を与えることだ。

CA'N TERRA

カン・テラ（大地の家）

Menorca, Spain 2018—2020

スペイン、メノルカ島

163

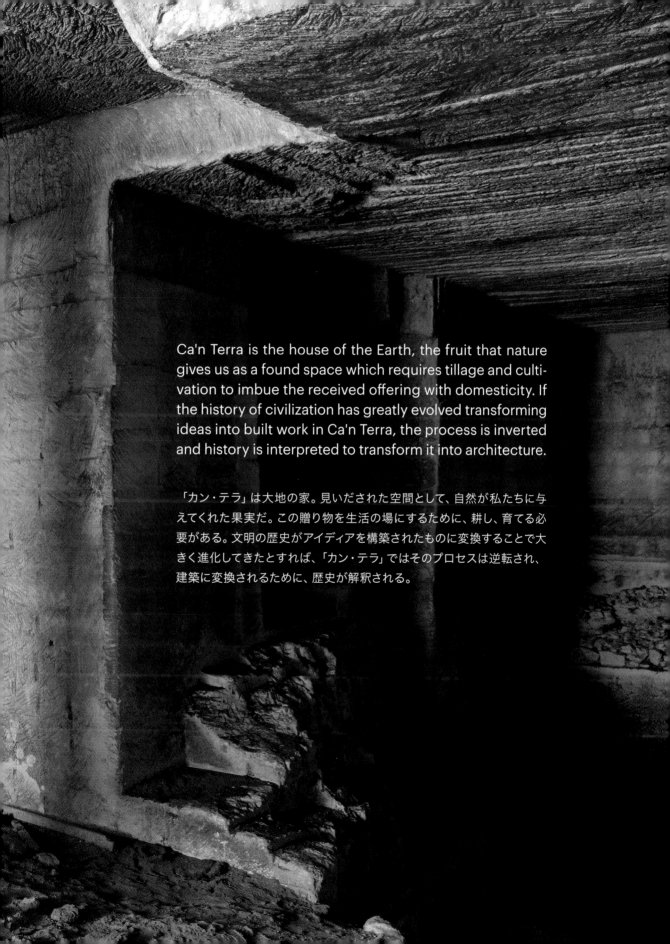

Ca'n Terra is the house of the Earth, the fruit that nature gives us as a found space which requires tillage and cultivation to imbue the received offering with domesticity. If the history of civilization has greatly evolved transforming ideas into built work in Ca'n Terra, the process is inverted and history is interpreted to transform it into architecture.

「カン・テラ」は大地の家。見いだされた空間として、自然が私たちに与えてくれた果実だ。この贈り物を生活の場にするために、耕し、育てる必要がある。文明の歴史がアイディアを構築されたものに変換することで大きく進化してきたとすれば、「カン・テラ」ではそのプロセスは逆転され、建築に変換されるために、歴史が解釈される。

Floor Plan
平面俯瞰図

0   20 m

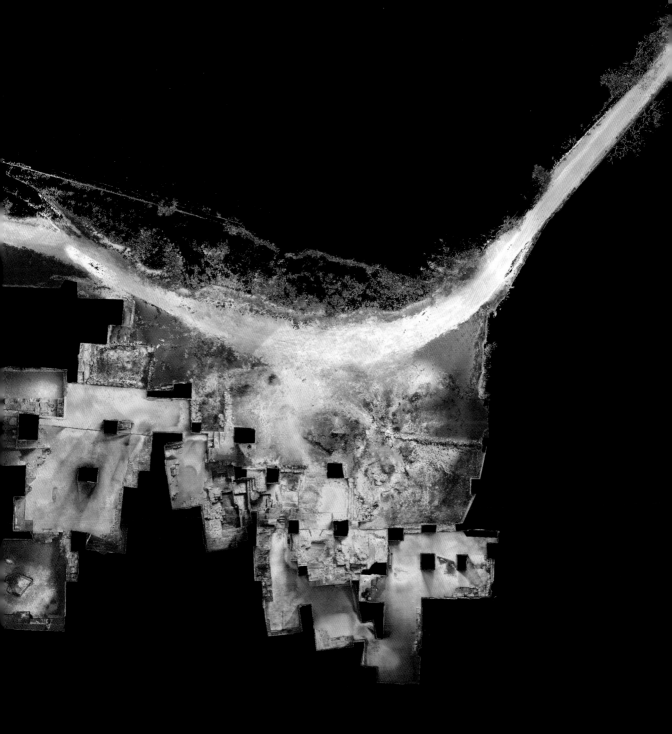

The transfer from drawing to built mass gives way to the translation of given matter to digital data through the architectural reading of a geological discovery.

ここでは、図面を構築されたマッスに変換するのではなく、大地から得た発見を建築的に読み取ることで、そこにある物質をデジタルデータに変換している。

The discovered space has industrial logic as a former Mares stone quarry, artistic potential as sublime cavern carved by hand, and mineral nature as extract of the stony landscape on the island of Menorca. Finding this excavated space in the guts of the earth and reinventing its use implies writing a new story that can rescue it from its abandonment.

発見された空間は、かつてのマレス石の採石場としての産業的論理と、手で彫られた荘厳な洞窟としての芸術的な可能性、そしてメノルカ島の石のランドスケープから抽出された鉱物としての性質をもつ。この掘り出された空間を大地の奥深くに見いだし、その使い方を新たに考え直すことは、見捨てられていた空間を救い出すための新しい物語を書くことを意味する。

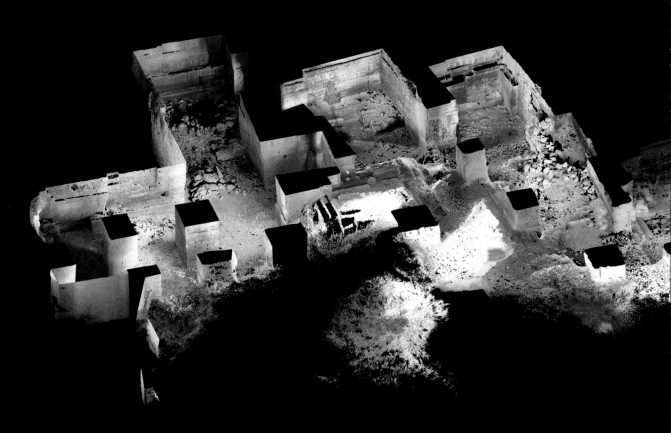

As a first contact, we enter the space like explorers would do, equipped with the technology that expands our vision in the dark; throwing millions of laser points on the wrinkles of the continuous stone surface we register with millimetric precision on the solid structure that was built for us and is now ready to be polished and inhabited. Behind the scan are the architect's eyes, directing, interpreting and creating the space again.

私たちのために築かれ、今ではいつでも磨き上げられて生活を受け入れられる状態にある重厚な構造物を初めて訪れたとき、私たちは探検家がするように暗視スコープを装備して、その空間に入った。そして連続する石の表面の細かい襞にレーザー光線を何百万回も連続照射してスキャンし、ミリ単位の精度で記録をした。スキャナーを背後で操る建築家の眼が、指示し、解釈し、その空間を再び創造したのだ。

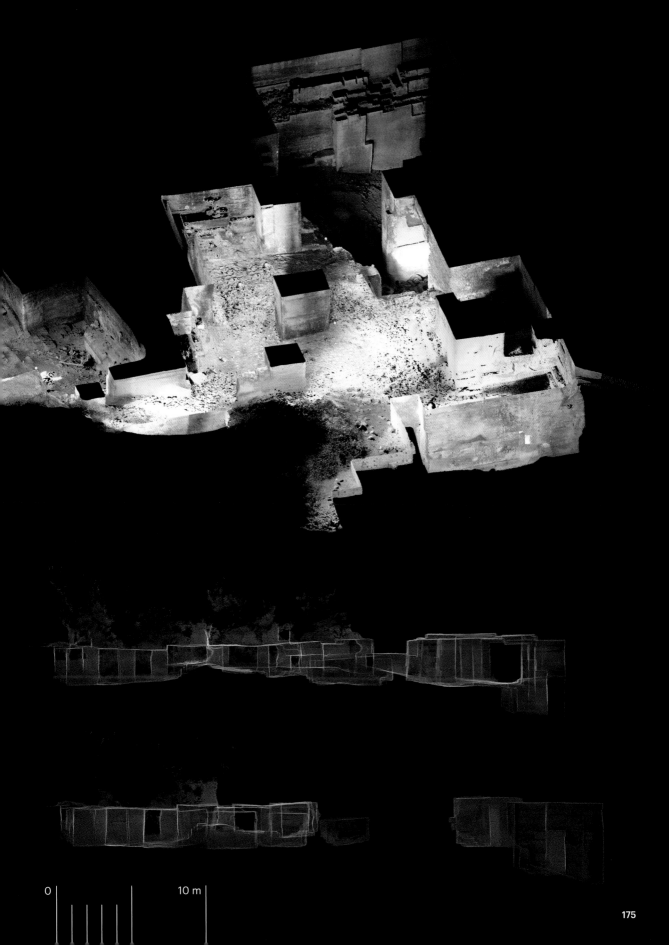

0   10 m

Architecture is built with air and light, introducing habitability where there is only darkness.

建築は空気と光で構築され、暗闇しかないところに居住性をもたらす。

The discovery is considered a new work. With minimal intervention and sensible actions, Architecture emerges and we are able to inhabit it.

私たちが発見したものは、新しい作品とみなされる。最小限の介入と思慮深い行動によって、建築が現れ、私たちはそこをすみかとすることができる。

In lieu of an imposing action, the kind that architecture often exerts on the environment, we propose a trip deep into the interior being of matter, and recognize the freedom with which it gives us spaces to live.

建築が環境に対して押し付けがちな行為の代わりに、物質の奥深くへと旅し、そこに私たちに生活空間を与えてくれる自由を見いだすことを提案したい。

THE ARCHITECTURE OF ENSAMBLE STUDIO

Ryue Nishizawa, Architect

I believe I first met Antón García-Abril and Débora Mesa in Madrid in the winter, in early 2010. I was on a trip in search of potential exhibitors for the Venice Architecture Biennial that year and was visiting their Madrid studio. I remember it being crammed with models large and small of projects they were in the midst of—the Telcel Theatre in Mexico, The Truffle, and the Berklee Tower of Music, built by piling precast I-beams, come to mind. Subsequently I attended three of their presentations in China, Japan, and Italy, and became further acquainted with their projects through magazines and the Internet. I also visited Hemeroscopium House, a residence they built in the Madrid suburbs. In fact, that was the only time I have actually seen their architecture with my own eyes. Though that makes any generalizations I might propose about their work highly suspect, I will try to articulate my impressions of it here.

The first word that occurs to me about their architecture is "power." When I visited the house in Madrid, my experience of its space conjured up an image of power. I cannot express exactly what sort of power—perhaps of human beings, perhaps of architecture. Or perhaps it is not a power of something specific, but simply, purely, power. In their work I sense power itself appearing before our eyes in the form of architecture. The sensation is one of "power emerging from within." This is not power of the outward, relative kind measured in social relationships, as when we speak of an influential politician or a strong fighter.

Rather, it is an internal, autonomous power that emanates from the deepest recesses of a human being. In the architecture of Ensamble Studio, power informs the structure, the shape, the space. My impression is that this is achieved through an extremely straightforward process.

The second thing I want to say about the work of García-Abril and Mesa is that in all of their projects, I see them directly responding to a question that certain architects seem to confront in their practice: "What is architecture?" Most structures we see around us, whether commercial buildings or art museums, can be designed without ever addressing this question. And indeed, most architects contemplate how architecture can be used, or how it can be built, rather than ask themselves what architecture itself is. However, when I view the work of Ensamble Studio—whether it is The Truffle, or Hemeroscopium House, or Ca'n Terra, a residence they created from an abandoned quarry on the island of Menorca—I see the construction method itself realized as an architectural space, and this gives me the impression that they have an innate desire to create architecture that answers the question, "What is architecture?" One senses that their answer is in their construction method, which they present as if to say, "This is what architecture is."

Louis Kahn once declared that "what" precedes "how."[1] One of the major negative legacies of modernist architecture was the proliferation, in the wake of the world's loss of so many structures in the two World Wars, of theories of "how" instead of "what" to build. It was in reaction to this state of affairs that Kahn stressed the importance of the "what" of architecture over the "how." Kahn's statement could be called historical for a number of reasons. One was as a critique of modernism, but it also strikes me as significant that this simple declaration put the world on notice that the era of "what" and "how" as one had ended, and an era in which they were clearly separated had begun. To borrow from Kahn's phrasing, the architecture of Ensamble Studio attempts to reintegrate the "what" and the "how." In my view, their work aims to demonstrate that these two aspects are fundamentally one, as was true in the past. Such is the degree to which their architecture is straightforwardly construction-oriented, directly translating their intentions vis-a-vis construction into method and thus into architectural space.

When I look at their architecture or listen to their presentations, I sense something extraordinary. I don't want to say "exorbitant," because their work is always thoroughly logical and their building methods make perfect sense. Yet at the same time their projects seem to unfold in ways that are highly unorthodox, even beyond the pale, one might say. That impression is usually strongest at times when I relate most sympathetically to what they are doing. What I sense is a human leaping—a life force that defies the sort of automatic, mechanistic logic that dictates the same results no matter who follows it. This leaping, which is inconceivable with mechanistic logic, occurs throughout the process of architectural creation. The architecture of García-Abril and Mesa is strong, solid, dynamic—yet no matter how industrial their building methods may be, or how much emphasis they may place on process, one always feels the presence there of the human will, and of human sensuality. Their work says to me that however much we may mechanize architecture, it is still a human endeavor. That is the aspect of their architecture, and of García-Abril and Mesa themselves, that I admire most.

[1] Louis Kahn, "The Room, the Street and Human Agreement," acceptance speech for the American Institute of Architects Gold Medal Award (1971)

アンサンブル・スタジオの建築について

西沢立衛、建築家

アントン・ガルシア゠アブリルとデボラ・メサのふたりに出会ったのは、私の記憶では２０１０年初め、冬のマドリッドにおいてであった。ベネチア・ビエンナーレ国際建築展の出展作家を探す旅行で、マドリッドの彼らのスタジオを訪れたのが、最初の出会いだった。彼らのスタジオではメキシコのプロジェクト[注1]や、トリュフのプロジェクト[注2]、Ｉ型プレキャストビームを積層したプロジェクト[注3]などが進行中で、大小の模型がスタジオ内に所狭しと並んでいたのを覚えている。その後私は、彼らのレクチャーを中国と日本、イタリアで３回聴講し、またインターネットや雑誌を通して、彼らのプロジェクトを何度か見た。私はまた、マドリッド郊外の住宅[注4]を訪れた。実は私は、彼らの建築を実際に見たのはその１回のみであり、彼らの建築を包括的に論じる力が私にあるかは疑問だが、私なりに感じたことをここで書いてみたい。

彼らの建築についてまず第一に私が思い浮かぶ言葉は、力だ。マドリッドの住宅を訪れて、その空間を経験して、私は力のイメージを感じた。その力が何なのか、私ははっきりと言葉にできないが、強いて言えば人間の力であるかもしれないし、建築の力かもしれない。もしかしたら、「なんとかの力」とか、そういうものではなくて、単に純粋に、力かもしれない。力が、そのまま建築となってわれわれの目の前に登場したような、そんな印象を私は彼らの建築に感じている。それは感覚的に言えば、「内側からやってきた力」のようなものだ。「政治家はえらい」とか「喧嘩に強い」というような、社会関係のなかで測られる相対的な、外的な力ではなく、人間の奥底からやってくる、内的で単独的な力だ。彼らの建築は、力が構築になり、形になり、空間になっている。それはたいへん直截的なやり方でそうなっている、と私は感じている。

私が彼らについて言いたい第2のことは、彼らは各建築プロジェクトを通して、建築設計においてある種の建築家がぶつかるであろう問題、つまり「建築とは何か?」という問いに、まっすぐ答えようとしているように見える点だ。世の中の建築の多くは、商業建築にしても美術館にしても、「建築とは何か?」を問わずにいくらでも作れてしまえるものだ。実際のところ多くの建築家は、「建築とは何か?」については特に考えず、むしろ「建築はどう使えるか?」または「どう作れるか?」の問題を考えようとしている。しかしアンサンブル・スタジオの建築に目を向けると、トリュフの住宅やマドリッドの住宅、またはメノルカ島の廃墟のプロジェクト(注5)などで、建設方法がそのまま建築空間として実体化するのを見るたびに私は、「建築とは何か」への答えとして自身の建築を存在させたいという願望が彼らの中にあるような、そういう印象を受ける。「建築とは何か」への答えとして、建築とはこれだ、と、構築方法を提示することで、答えにしようとしているように感じられる。ルイス・カーンはかつて、ホワットはハウに先駆する(注6)と言った。両大戦によって多くの建造物を失った世界は、「何を作るか」よりも「どう作るか」の理論を発展させてゆき、それはモダニズム建築が遺した大きな負の遺産のひとつとなった。それへの反省からカーンは、ホワット(建築とは何か)をハウ(どう作るか)より高い位置に置いた。カーンのこの発言が歴史的と言えるのは、モダニズム批判ということがひとつあるが、もうひとつ重要と私が感じる

のは、ホワットとハウがひとつのことであった時代が終わり、ホワットとハウが明確に区別される時代がはじまったことを、単純な言葉によって皆に知らしめたことだ。カーンのこの言葉を借用しつつ言うならば、アンサンブル・スタジオの建築は、ホワットとハウを再びつなげたものとして存在させようとしている。かつてそうであったように、そのふたつはそもそも同じひとつのことだと示そうとしている、と私には感じられる。それほど彼らの建築はストレートに構築的であり、構築への意思が、そのまま方法となり、また建築空間になっている。

私は彼らの建築を見たり、または彼らの講演会を聞くとき、どこか普通ではないとしばしば感じる。非常識と言いたいわけではなくて、そういう意味では彼らの建築はどれも論理的であり、むしろいつも筋の通った作られ方をしている。しかし、論理的であればあるほど、何かどこか突き抜けているというか、普通じゃない展開が起きていると感じる。そう感じるときはたいがい、私が彼らに共感しているときだ。私はそこに人間の跳躍を感じる。誰がやっても同じ答えに辿り着くような自動的で機械的な論理に従わない生命力が、そこにある。機械的論理ではおよそあり得ないような飛躍が、建築創造過程の随所にある。彼らの建築は強く重く、ダイナミックだが、彼らがどこまで工業的な作り方をしても、どこまで手順を重んじているとしても、そこには人間の意思があり、人間の官能性がある。建築はどこまで機械化しても、それはなお人間の技なのだと、彼らの建築が言っているように私には感じられる。このことは、私が彼らと彼らの建築を称賛する最大の部分だ。

(注1)　Telcel Theater
(注2)　The Truffle
(注3)　Berklee Tower of Music
(注4)　Hemeroscopium House
(注5)　Ca'n Terra
(注6)　ルイス・カーンによる講演会 "The Room, the street, and Human Agreement," American Institute of Architects Gold medal Award Address (1971) より

WORKS LIST 作品リスト

Musical Studies Center
音楽高等学校

Santiago de Compostela, Spain, 2003
Author 建築家: Ensamble Studio, Antón García-Abril **Project Team** プロジェクトチーム: Javier Cuesta (Building Engineer), Bernardo Angelini, Eduardo Martín Asunción, Arantxa Osés, Andrés Toledo, Guillermo Sevillano **Developer** デベロッパー: Santiago de Compostela's Consortium **Contractor** 施工者: O.H.L **Consultants** コンサルタント: Obradoiro Enxeñeiros (MEP), Jesús Huerga (Structure) **Built Area** 建築面積: 1,700 ㎡

📍 **Visitors' info** 見学案内
Address 住所: Rúa de Vista Alegre, 1 B, 15705 Santiago de Compostela, A Coruña (in the same park where SGAE HQ stands スペイン著作権協会本部がある公園内)
www.eaem.es

Auditorium and Music School
オーディトリアムと音楽学校

Medina del Campo, Valladolid, Spain, 2003
Author 建築家: Ensamble Studio, Antón García-Abril **Project Team** プロジェクトチーム: Javier Cuesta (Building Engineer) **Developer** デベロッパー: Medina del Campo City Council **Contractor** 施工者: O.H.L **Built Area** 建築面積: 2,400 ㎡

📍 **Visitors' info** 見学案内
Address 住所: Plaza Segovia, s/n, 47400 Medina del Campo, Valladolid
www.auditoriomedinadelcampo.es

Valdés Studio
バルデス・スタジオ

Madrid, Spain, 2004
Author 建築家: Ensamble Studio, Antón García-Abril **Project Team** プロジェクトチーム: Javier Cuesta (Building Engineer), Ignacio Marí, Johannes Gramse **Developer** デベロッパー: Manuel Valdés Blasco **Contractor** 施工者: Materia Inorgánica **Built Area** 建築面積: 900 ㎡

Martemar House
マルテマル・ハウス

Benahavis, Málaga, Spain, 2005
Author 建築家: Ensamble Studio, Antón García-Abril **Project Team** プロジェクトチーム: Javier Cuesta (Building Engineer), Guillermo Sevillano (Project Manager), Débora Mesa, Johannes Gramse, Claudia Gans, Jorge Consuegra, Jan Goebel **Developer** デベロッパー: Artime **Contractor** 施工者: Materia Inorgánica **Consultants** コンサルタント: Obradoiro Enxeñeiros (MEP), Jesús Huerga (Structure) **Built Area** 建築面積: 1,640 ㎡

SGAE Headquarters
スペイン著作権協会本部

Santiago de Compostela, Spain, 2007
Author 建築家: Ensamble Studio, Antón García-Abril **Project Team** プロジェクトチーム: Débora Mesa (Associate Architect), Javier Cuesta (Building Engineer), José Antonio Millán, Ricardo Sanz, Marina Otero, Elena Pérez, Helena Serrano, Jorge Consuegra, Andrés Toledo **Developer** デベロッパー: SGAE **Contractor** 施工者: Materia Inorgánica **Consultants** コンサルタント: Obradoiro Enxeñeiros (MEP), Jesús Huerga (Structure) **Quarry** 採石場: Granichán **Built Area** 建築面積: 3,000 ㎡

📍 **Visitors' info** 見学案内
Address 住所: Rúa das Salvadas, 2 A, 15705 Santiago de Compostela, A Coruña (in the same park where the Musical Studies Center stands 音楽高等学校がある公園内) **www.sgae.es**

Hemeroscopium House
ヘメロスコピウム・ハウス

Las Rozas, Madrid, Spain, 2008
Author 建築家: Ensamble Studio, Antón García-Abril **Project Team** プロジェクトチーム: Javier Cuesta (Building Engineer), Débora Mesa (Associate Architect), Elena Pérez (Project Manager), Marina Otero, Ricardo Sanz, Jorge Consuegra **Developer** デベロッパー: Hemeroscopium **Contractor** 施工者: Materia Inorgánica **Consultants** コンサルタント: Obradoiro Enxeñeiros (MEP), Jesús Huerga (Structure) **Built Area** 建築面積: 400 ㎡

Balancing Act
バランシング・アクト

Venice Biennale, Venice, Italy, 2010
Author 建築家: Ensamble Studio, Antón García-Abril **Project Team** プロジェクトチーム: Javier Cuesta, Débora Mesa, Ricardo Sanz, Alba Cortes, Juan Ruiz, Tomaso Boano, Federico Letizia **Sponsor** スポンサー: Positive City Foundation

Museum of America
アメリカ博物館

Salamanca, Spain, 2010
Author 建築家: Ensamble Studio, Antón García-Abril **Project Team** プロジェクトチーム: Javier Cuesta (Building Engineer), Ricardo Sanz (Project Manager), Débora Mesa **Developer** デベロッパー: Caja de Ahorros de Salamanca y Soria
Contractor 施工者: Isolux Corsán
Consultants コンサルタント: Urculo Engineering (MEP), Jesús Huerga (Structure) **Collaborating companies** 協力企業: Euroclima, Targetti **Built Area** 建築面積: 1,250 m²

The Truffle　トリュフ

Costa da Morte, Spain, 2010
Author 建築家: Ensamble Studio, Antón García-Abril **Project Team** プロジェクトチーム: Javier Cuesta (Building Engineer), Débora Mesa (Associate Architect), Ricardo Sanz (Project Manager)
Developer デベロッパー: Ensamble Studio
Contractor 施工者: Materia Inorgánica
Consultants コンサルタント: Obradoiro Enxeñeiros (MEP), Jesús Huerga (Structure) **Collaborating companies** 協力企業: Galicorte, Macías Derribos, Suministros Zurich, Ganadería Paulina, Franchetau **Built Area** 建築面積: 25 m²

Reader's House
リーダーズ・ハウス

Old Slaughterhouse, Madrid, Spain, 2012
Author 建築家: Ensamble Studio, Antón García-Abril & Débora Mesa
Project Team プロジェクトチーム: Javier Cuesta (Building Engineer), Marina Otero (Project Manager), Elena Pérez, Ricardo Sanz, Alba Cortés **Developer** デベロッパー: Fundación Germán Sánchez Ruipérez
Contractor 施工者: Ferrovial **Consultants** コンサルタント: Urculo Engineering (MEP), Jesús Huerga (Structure) **Collaborating companies** 協力企業: Prainsa **Built Area** 建築面積: 7,500 m²

 Visitors' info 見学案内
Address 住所: Paseo de la Chopera, 14, 28045 Madrid
www.mataderomadrid.org/instituciones/casa-del-lector

The Cloud　ザ・クラウド

Madrid, Spain, 2012
Author 建築家: Ensamble Studio, Antón García-Abril & Débora Mesa **Project Team** プロジェクトチーム: Javier Cuesta (Building Engineer), Sara Nunes, Valentina Marchetti, Karlien Van der Linden, Aukje Gossens, José María Lavena **Developer** デベロッパー: Fundación Germán Sánchez Ruipérez.

 **Visitors' info** 見学案内
Installation located in the Reader's House リーダーズ・ハウスに設置されたインスタレーション

Telcel Theater　テルセル劇場

Mexico City, Mexico, 2012
Author 建築家: Ensamble Studio, Antón García-Abril **Project Team** プロジェクトチーム: Javier Cuesta (Building Engineer), Débora Mesa (Associate Architect), Elena Pérez (Associate Architect), Alba Cortés (Project Manager), Joaquín Gallegos, Alba Beroiz, Jaime Alcayde, Cristina Moya, Juan Ruiz Antón, Tomaso Boano, Federico Letizia **Developer** デベロッパー: SGAE - GRUPO CARSO **Project Manager** プロジェクトマネージャー: INPROS **Contractor** 施工者: GRUPO PC **Consultants** コンサルタント: Colinas de Buen (Structure) **Built Area** 建築面積: 11,500 m²

Visitors' info 見学案内
Address 住所: Blvd. Miguel de Cervantes Saavedra 386, Amp Granada, Miguel Hidalgo, 11529 Ciudad de México, Mexico
https://teatrotelcel.com.mx/

BUS:STOP
バス停

Krumbach, Austria, 2013
Author 建築家: Ensamble Studio, Antón García-Abril & Débora Mesa
Project Team プロジェクトチーム: Evelyn Ting, Lap Hang Hao **Developer** デベロッパー: Verein Kultur Krumbach
Consultants コンサルタント: Ensamble Studio, Mader Flatz Bregenz (Structure)
Local architect ローカルアーキテクト: Dietrich|Untertrifaller Architekten
Collaborating companies 協力企業: Zimmerei Gerhard Berchtold Schwarzenberg **Sponsor** スポンサー: Hypo Vorarlberg **Built Area** 建築面積: 7.5 m²

📍 **Visitors' info** 見学案内
Address 住所: Unterkrumbach 203-224; 6942 Krumbach, Austria

CUBIC IGLOO
キュービック・イグルー

MIT Campus, Cambridge, Massachusetts, USA, 2013
Author 建築家: Ensamble Studio & MIT-POPlab **Principal investigators** 主任研究員: Antón García-Abril & Débora Mesa **Project team** プロジェクトチーム: Javier Cuesta, Ricardo Sanz, Marie Benaboud, Elisa Giusti, Borja Soriano, Dario Bruni, Chiara de Crescenzo, Petros Marmaras, Alvaro Catalan **MIT students** MIT学生: Kenny Chan, Jinhui Huang, Yi Hou, Shaoyi Liang **Sponsor** スポンサー: Sidney E. Frank Foundation **Built Area** 建築面積: 23 m²

Cyclopean House
シクロピアン・ハウス

Brookline, Boston, Massachusetts, USA, 2015
Author 建築家: Ensamble Studio, Antón García-Abril & Débora Mesa **Project Team** プロジェクトチーム: Javier Cuesta (Building Engineer), Ricardo Sanz (Project Manager), Borja Soriano, Massimo Loia, Walter Cuccuru. Valentina Giacomini, Marietta Spyrou, Juanjo Fernández, Federica Zunino, Marian Stanislav, Chung-Wen Wu, Yannis Karababas **Developer** デベロッパー: Ensamble Studio **Fabricator/Contractor** 製作者/施工者: Materia Inorgánica **Consultants** コンサルタント: Urculo Engineering (MEP), Jesús Huerga (Structure) **Built Area** 建築面積: 240 m²

Structures of Landscape - Tippet Rise Art Center
ランドスケープの構造体
ティペット・ライズ・アート・センター

Fishtail, Montana, USA, 2016
Author 建築家: Ensamble Studio, Antón García-Abril & Débora Mesa **Project Team** プロジェクトチーム: Javier Cuesta (Building Engineer), Ricardo Sanz (Project Manager), Massimo Loia, Simone Cavallo, Borja Soriano **Developer** デベロッパー: Tippet Rise, Sidney E. Frank Foundation **Contractor** 施工者: O.S.M **Consultants** コンサルタント: Jesús Huerga, Beaudette (Structure) **Collaborating Companies** 協力企業: David and Sons, CMG, Mountain West Steel **Built Area** 建築面積: 4,600 ha (Masterplan), 600 m² (Structures)

📍 **Visitors' info** 見学案内
Address 住所: 96 S. Grove Creek Rd. Fishtail, MT 59028 Montana, USA. You can enjoy hiking, biking, music concerts and more events. Closed in Winter. ハイキング、自転車、音楽コンサートやさまざまなイベントが楽しめる。冬季休園。**https://tippetrise.org/**

Supraextructures vs. Structures of Landscape
超構造体 (スーパーストラクチャー) 対 ランドスケープの構造体

Venice Biennale, Venice, Italy, 2016
Author 建築家: Ensamble Studio, Antón García-Abril & Débora Mesa **Project Team** プロジェクトチーム: Javier Cuesta, Borja Soriano, Simone Cavallo, Massimo Loia, Pablo Manso, Walter Cuccuru, João Alves

Big Bang Tower
ビッグバンの塔

Chicago Architecture Biennale, Chicago, USA, 2017
Author 建築家: Ensamble Studio, Antón García-Abril & Débora Mesa
Project Team プロジェクトチーム: Javier Cuesta, Borja Soriano, Simone Cavallo, Massimo Loia, Silvia Sáez, Joakim Aslund **Developer** デベロッパー: Chicago Architecture Biennale **Consultants** コンサルタント: Torroja Engineering (Structure) **Fabricator** 製作者: Ravenswood Studio

Towers of Landscape
ランドスケープの塔

Biennale d'Architecture d'Orléans, Orléans, France, 2017
Author 建築家: Ensamble Studio, Antón García-Abril & Débora Mesa **Project Team** プロジェクトチーム: Javier Cuesta, Borja Soriano, Alvaro Catalan, Michele Matteo Marcotulli, Massimo Loia, Areej Alchalabi, Monica Acosta

Ensamble Place
アンサンブル・プレイス

Madrid, Spain, Ensamble Studio, Antón García-Abril & Débora Mesa **Project Team** プロジェクトチーム: Javier Cuesta (Building Engineer), Ricardo Sanz, Borja Soriano, Alvaro Catalan, Petros Marmaras, Oscar Carballal, Pablo Manso, Marcos Jiménez **Developer** デベロッパー: Ensamble Studio **Contractor** 施工者: Materia Inorgánica **Consultants** コンサルタント: Jesús Huerga (Structure) **Built Area** 建築面積: 350 m²

Petrified River
ペトリファイド・リバー (石化した川)

Cooper Hewitt Smithsonian Design Museum, New York, New York, USA, 2019
Author 建築家: Ensamble Studio, Antón García-Abril & Débora Mesa **Project Team** プロジェクトチーム: Javier Cuesta (Building Engineer), Borja Soriano (Project Manager), Massimo Loia, Mengyuan Cao, Alvaro Catalan, Mónica Acosta, Niccolo Ciaccheri, Federico Lepre, Marco Antrodicchia, Arianna Sebastianni, Sebastian Zapata, Riccardo Gialloreto, Pinjung Chen, Yun Tso Chung **Client** 施主: Cooper Hewitt Smithsonian Design Museum, CUBE Design Museum **Sponsors** スポンサー: Sidney E. Frank Foundation **Consultants** コンサルタント: Torroja Engineering (Structure)

Ca'n Terra   カン・テラ (大地の家)
Menorca, Spain, 2020
Author 建築家: Ensamble Studio, Antón García-Abril & Débora Mesa **Project Team** プロジェクトチーム: Javier Cuesta (Building Engineer), Borja Soriano (Project Manager), Claudia Armas, Alvaro Catalan, Massimo Loia, Marco Antrodicchia, Sebastián Zapata, Arianna Sebastiani, Ekam Sahni, Yu-Ting Li, Joel Kim, Gonzalo Peña, Barbara Doroszuk, Yvonne Asiimwe, Mónica Acosta **Developer** デベロッパー: Ensamble Studio **Contractor** 施工者: Ensamble Studio **Consultants** コンサルタント: Urculo Engineering (MEP) **Built Area** 建築面積: 1,000 m²

Ensamble Fabrica
アンサンブル・ファブリカ

Madrid, Spain, 2019
Author 建築家: Antón García-Abril & Débora Mesa **Project Team** プロジェクトチーム: Javier Cuesta (Building Engineer), Borja Soriano, Niccolo Ciaccheri, Federico Lepre, Massimo Loia, Alvaro Catalan, Mengyuan Cao, María José Carrillo, Mónica Acosta, Elyse Khoury, Marco Antrodicchia, Arianna Sebastiani **Developer** デベロッパー: Ensamble Studio **Contractor** 施工者: Materia Inorgánica **Consultants:** コンサルタント: Urculo Engineering (MEP), Jesús Huerga (Structure) **Built Area** 建築面積: 1,150 m²

The Tent
テント

Costa da Morte, Spain, 2020
Author 建築家: Antón García-Abril & Débora Mesa **Project Team** プロジェクトチーム: Javier Cuesta (Building Engineer), Borja Soriano, Alvaro Catalan, Fernando González **Developer** デベロッパー: Ensamble Studio **Contractor** 施工者: Materia Inorgánica **Consultants** コンサルタント: Jesús Huerga (Structure) **Built Area** 建築面積: 35 m²

PROFILE

Ensamble Studio is a cross-disciplinary team founded in 2000 and is led by architects Antón García-Abril and Débora Mesa. Balancing imagination and reality, art and science, their works adopt typologies, technologies and methodologies to address issues as diverse as construction of the landscapes or prefabrication of houses. From their early works—*SGAE Headquarters* in Santiago de Compostela, *Hemeroscopium House* in Madrid or *The Truffle* in Costa da Morte, Spain—to their most recent—*Ensamble Fabrica* in Madrid and *Ca'n Terra* in Menorca, Spain—, every project creats space for experimentation aiming to advance their field. Currently, through their startup *WoHo,* they are invested in increasing the quality of architecture while making it more affordable by integrating offsite technologies. Their new research and fabrication facility in Madrid, *Ensamble Fabrica*, was established to support this endeavor. Antón and Débora are committed to sharing ideas and cultivating synergies between professional and academic worlds through teaching, lecturing and researching: she is the Ventulett Chair in Architectural Design at Georgia Tech and he is a Professor at MIT, where they co-founded the POPlab—*Prototypes of Prefabrication Laboratory*—in 2012.

プロフィール

アンサンブル・スタジオは、2000年に設立された、建築家のアントン・ガルシア＝アブリルとデボラ・メサが率いる職能横断型チームである。彼らの作品は、想像と現実、芸術と科学のバランスをとりながら、タイポロジー、技術、方法論を刷新し、ランドスケープの構築から住宅のプレファブリケーションまで、さまざまな課題に取り組んでいる。スペインでは「スペイン著作権協会本部」(サンティアゴ・デ・コンポステーラ)、「ヘメロスコピウム・ハウス」(マドリッド)、「トリュフ」(コスタ・ダ・モルテ) などの初期の作品から、「アンサンブル・ファブリカ」(マドリッド) や「カン・テラ (大地の家)」(メノルカ島) などの最新作に至るまで、すべてのプロジェクトにおいて、活動領域をさらに発展させることを目指して、実験の場を設けている。現在、彼らはスタートアップ「WoHo」を通じて、現場外の技術を統合することで質の高い建築をより安価に提供するための事業に投資している。この試みを支援する目的で、新しい研究・製造施設「アンサンブル・ファブリカ」をマドリッドに設立した。アントンとデボラは、教育、講演、研究を横断しながらアイディアを共有し、建築業界と学術界の相乗効果を高めることに尽力している。デボラはジョージア工科大学、アントンはマサチューセッツ工科大学 (MIT) で教鞭をとる。2012年に、MITでPOPLabを共同設立した。

Photographic images　写真
Iwan Baan　イワン・バーン
(p. 17, pp. 20–27, p. 29, pp. 32–41, pp. 49–53, pp. 56–57, pp. 72–73, p. 77, pp. 78–79, p. 81, pp. 84–88,
pp. 153–156, pp. 158–173, pp. 178–191, Backcover)
Ensamble Studio　アンサンブル・スタジオ (All photos except those listed above 上記以外)

Translation, English to Japanese　和訳
Kazuko Sakamoto　坂本和子

Translation, Japanese to English　英訳
Alan Gleason　アラン・グリースン (pp. 194–195)

English proofreading　英文校正
Harutaka Oribe　織部晴崇

Japanese proofreading　日本語校正
Ouraido K.K.　株式会社 鷗来堂

Coordination　編集協力
Alvaro Catalan, Ensamble Studio　アルヴァロ・カタラン、アンサンブル・スタジオ
Tomoko Sakamoto　坂本知子

大地の建築　アンサンブル・スタジオ

2021年6月8日　初版第1刷発行
2022年2月10日　初版第2刷発行

著者　アンサンブル・スタジオ：
　　　アントン・ガルシア＝アブリル、デボラ・メサ
発行者　伊藤剛士
発行所　TOTO出版 (TOTO株式会社)
〒107-0062 東京都港区南青山1-24-3 TOTO乃木坂ビル2F
[営業] TEL 03-3402-7138　FAX 03-3402-7187
[編集] TEL 03-3497-1010
URL https://jp.toto.com/publishing

ブック・デザイン spread (坂本知子、 ダビッド・ロレンテ)
印刷・製本 株式会社 サンニチ印刷
落丁本・乱丁本はお取り替えいたします。

Printed in Japan
ISBN 978-4-88706-390-7